The Mother
The Soldier
The Activist

Kathy Greggs

Copyright © 2023

All Rights Reserved

Dedication

Even though they are no longer alive, their memories still control how I live.

Former Councilmember CW3 (R) Thedore Mohn

November 6, 1963 - August 13, 2023

'Soldier for Life'

Thank you for your mentorship and guidance to me and my Fayetteville PACT members.

DODEA (R) Teacher, Author, and Entrepreneur Ruby Lee Jones

July 12, 1947- July 29, 2023

I want to thank Ruby Jones, who loved me so much and taught me the value of working hard. Ruby, thank you so much; I will never forget you.

For the lives lost because of Police Brutality in Fayetteville 'Can Do City,' Lumberton and Hope Mills, NC.

Nijza Hagans (Fayetteville Police Department)

On January 24, 2013, a 22-year-old black man was pulled over by police officer Aaron Hunt for running a red light and making "several furtive driving maneuvers such as darting onto a neighborhood street and into a driveway," as stated in a memo by Cumberland County's district attorney, Billy West. Despite being unarmed, Hunt claimed that he saw Hagans reach aggressively for a gun in his pants pocket as he opened his car door. West's memo, which can be found here,[1] concluded that Hunt's response was considered 'lawful and measured. Following a request for investigation from Fayetteville PACT, the DOJ conducted an inquiry, **but no charges were ever filed.**

Treva Smutherman (Fayetteville Police Department)

On November 2, 2019, a 31-year-old black man was shot and killed by a Fayetteville detective at the Cape Fear Valley hospital while in custody with the Cumberland County Sheriff's Department. According to the police, Smutherman attempted to take a deputy's weapon, leading to a struggle.

A video recorded by a patient shows Smutherman pleading for his life, saying, "I don't wanna die, don't shoot me in my face," while struggling with an officer.

In the video, a nurse can be heard instructing the detective to shoot Smutherman and then telling others not to treat him. Fayetteville PACT requested an investigation from the DOJ, **but no charges were ever filed.**

Joshua Oxendine (Cumberland County Sheriff's Department)
September 12, 2019

Unarmed 35-year-old Native American man died in the custody of the Cumberland County Sheriff's Department. The deputy said the man then started beating on the hood of his patrol car and refused to obey commands.

---

[1] https://www.documentcloud.org/documents/2082056-response-to-in quiry.html

The deputy said he took the man to the ground and handcuffed him. After the man was detained, Fayetteville officers noticed that he was no longer breathing. They performed CPR and called for emergency medical assistance but were not able to revive him. Fayetteville PACT requested an investigation from the DOJ. ***No charges were ever filed.***

Kevin Grissett (Fayetteville Police Department) Hope Mills February 1, 2014.

An unarmed 25-year-old Black man was shot five times in the back by Jacob Pfeffer, an off-duty Hope Mills police Driving an unmarked car while pursuing a vehicle, Pfeffer unloaded his weapon into Kevin's back once the car he was driving came to a stop. Even before this unjustified and suspicious use of deadly force, Pfeffer had a troubled record that included being placed on administrative leave for communicating threats as well as other suspicious activities. The family has been seeking justice for Kevin for more than nine years. Fayetteville PACT requested an investigation from the DOJ. ***No charges were ever filed.***

Lawrence Graham III (Fayetteville Police Department)
May 19, 2013

20-year-old Fayetteville man was paralyzed and later died after being shot in the back by former Fayetteville Police Officer Denton Little. Lawrence was riding with his friend, 24-year-old Antoine Morrell Willis when they were pulled over by Fayetteville Police Officer Philip Burlingame for tinted windows. Claiming the young men were acting "suspiciously," Burlingame called for back-up. Little responded Fayetteville Police held back the dash cam video of the incident for over three years, finally releasing it in September 2016. Watching the video, we learn that Ofc. Burlingame had removed Willis, the driver, from the vehicle and taken him outside the dashboard's view. At this point, Lawrence remained in the passenger seat of the vehicle, and Ofc. Little stood outside the passenger door, next to Lawrence. After fighting to survive and adapt to life as a paraplegic, Lawrence died on July 2, 2013; Fayetteville PACT requested an investigation from the DOJ. *No charges were ever filed.*

Jada Johnson (Fayetteville Police Department)
July 01, 2022

22-year-old black female sustained 17 gunshot wounds, including two to her head, according to the autopsy report. The report revealed that Johnson was shot twice in the head, once in the right forearm, three times in the shoulder area, and 11 times in the torso, with some shots entering through the back.

Additionally, the report mentioned minor blunt force injuries such as contusions, abrasions, and minute tissue tears on the arms, wrists, and right hand.At 9:46 p.m., Johnson placed a second call to 911, reporting that men were breaking into her house. Her voice was captured in both the second call and the original recording, where her grandmother remained on the phone with 911. Five minutes later, Johnson made a third call, during which she expressed the belief that law enforcement was involved with her ex-boyfriend and stated that she would go outside and talk to the men she believed were breaking in.

The dispatch logs noted that Johnson had a 'long history' of mental illness and had made ten calls on June 29. Officer Zacharius Borom, identified by the Fayetteville Police Department as the shooter, and Sgt. Timothy Rugg, who was also inside the home at the time of the shooting, were involved in the incident. The North Carolina prosecutor decided not to press charges. Following the incident, Fayetteville PACT requested an investigation from the DOJ. **No charges were ever filed.**

Adrian Roberts (Cumberland County Sheriff)
August 18, 2020

Adrian Roberts, a 37-year-old disabled combat war veteran, regularly recorded his interactions with the Cumberland County Sheriff's Department. He had posted multiple videos on Facebook on the day of his death

. These videos depict Adrian running inside and locking the door each time armed deputies arrived at his home, expressing fear by saying, "I'm scared of you guys." Due to his service-related PTSD, Adrian had a fear of guns and explicitly asked the deputies not to come to his house armed and requested them to leave.

The deputies informed Ms. Roberts that only one officer discharged his weapon, and the official report stated that Adrian was shot once. However, Adrian's death certificate indicates that he died from multiple gunshot wounds. Although a pocketknife was found on Adrian's body, the Sheriff's Department claimed it was a machete. Following the incident, Fayetteville PACT requested an investigation from the DOJ. **No charges were ever filed.**

John Hare (Cumberland County Sheriff Deputy)
October 6, 2020

A 62-year-old white military combat veteran was involved in an incident when deputies were conducting a wellness check on a suicidal man. According to sources close to the investigation, the man, identified as Hare, aimed his gun at the deputies and refused to put it down. As a result, he was shot by the deputies. Fayetteville PACT requested an investigation from the DOJ. **No charges were ever filed.**

Jason Walker (Off Duty Cumberland County Sheriff Deputy)
January 08, 2022

37-year-old unarmed black man was involved in an incident with Lt. Jeffrey Hash of the Cumberland County Sheriff's Office. Hash reported to the dispatcher that the man had jumped on his vehicle and broken his windshield, after which he shot him. Hash claimed that the man, identified as Jason Walker, had come running across Bingham Drive towards his vehicle. The autopsy revealed that Jason had wounds on his elbows and was shot in the back of the headfirst, followed by four shots while he was face down on the ground.

The North Carolina prosecutor did not press charges against Lt. Hash, citing the stand-your-ground law of North Carolina. Lt. Hash continues to be on duty at the Cumberland County Sheriff's Department, and the Department of Justice was not involved in the case. Fayetteville PACT requested an investigation from the DOJ. **No charges were ever filed.**

Wendy Sutton (Cumberland County Detention Center)

July 20, 2020

29-year-old white female was found in her cell. Inmates stated they heard her screaming for help, but no assistance was given; she was found unresponsive in her cell. The autopsy revealed she suffered from blunt force trauma to the back of the head, and she had bruises and marks around her chest area. Cumberland County Sheriff's Department never commented on the death. Fayetteville PACT requested an investigation from the DOJ. *No charges were ever filed.*

Matthew Oxendine (Robeson County Sheriff's Department)

January 21, 2021

Unarmed 46-year-old Native American man, Matt, had a history of mental illness. After losing his wife in 2016, he went into a state of grief and deep depression that led to him being hospitalized for a week and medicated.

The night he was killed, Matt had made a 911 call for medical assistance. When the sheriff's deputies arrived, he told them he was fine, and they should leave. Robeson County Sheriff's deputies used both high-powered rifles and handguns to shoot Matt 30 times, blowing a large hole in the left side of his face, shattering his shoulder blade, tearing off most of his left arm, and lodging numerous bullets in his spine. Fayetteville PACT requested an investigation from the DOJ. *No charges were ever filed.*

Justin Livesay (Fayetteville Police Department)
September 02, 2022

Officers responded to reports of an armed and suicidal individual at a mobile home park on Hickory View Court. Upon arrival, officers encountered a 40-year-old man who was armed with two knives. According to officials, there were five officers present who attempted to deescalate the situation.

They issued verbal commands for the man to drop the knives and utilized a taser. However, despite initially going down, the man managed to get back up while still armed with the knives and continued to advance towards the officers. As a result, the officers discharged their firearms, and the man was fatally shot at the scene.

Following the incident, Fayetteville PACT requested an investigation from the DOJ, **but no charges were filed.**

Organizations that assisted with building Fayetteville PACT

North Carolina Black Leaders Organizing Collective

Your partnership has been a catalyst for growth and progress. We couldn't have done it without you. Thank you!

Black Voters Matter NC

We are immensely grateful for the opportunity to work with you. Your insight and expertise have made a significant impact on our journey.

Ivanna Gonzalez (Former NC Blueprint Organizer)

Your belief in our mission fuels our motivation to excel. We are grateful for the confidence you've shown in us.

NC National Organization for Women (Fayetteville Chapter)

Our success is a testament to the exceptional relationships we have built. Thank you for being a vital link in our chain of accomplishments.

New Black Panthers Party (Lumberton, NC)

Your exceptional leadership and vision have been transformative for our organization. We are grateful for your guidance and the positive impact you have made.

Stop Killing US.org

Thank you for your unwavering belief in our team and the opportunities you provide for growth. We are honored to have you as a trusted partner.

People's Budget NC

Your support and encouragement have been invaluable, and we appreciate your continued partnership.

NC Medicare for All Coalition

Your support and camaraderie made it an unforgettable experience for all of us.

Cypress Action Fund

We extend our deepest appreciation for your ongoing commitment to our shared vision. Your dedication has been the driving force behind our accomplishments.

Domestic Violence Rally CEO Cynthia Hale

Thank you for your commitment to excellence and for pushing us to continually raise the bar. Your high standards have helped us achieve remarkable outcomes.

Dylan Dodson, CEO of Dodson Development

It's with genuine appreciation that we acknowledge your exceptional teamwork. Together, we've achieved remarkable milestones.

The Kool Spot Podcast

Thank you for going above and beyond in your efforts. Your commitment to excellence inspires us all.

Black Business Expo CEO Expo Dr. Eric Kelly

A sincere thank you for being a cornerstone of our success. Your valuable contributions have made a significant impact on our organization.

Cumberland County Organizing Against Racism

Your unwavering support and encouragement mean a lot to our team.

The NC Carolina Beat News (Gerald Jackson)

The positive exposure you gave our firm on the local news segment provided the community with a nice introduction to our goals and services.

City View NC (Columnist Bill Kirby Jr.)

We feel that your journalistic work is in the best tradition.

Paul Woolverton (Former Reporter for Fayetteville Observer)

Our organization appreciates your clear and accurate reporting.

Lexi Solmon (Government Watchdog Reporter Fayetteville Observer)

We sincerely appreciate your excellent coverage of Fayetteville PACT and police accountability topics.

Common (Rapper, Actor, Author, Activist)

Common is amongthe guests to attend them White House's celebration of American poetry, which is being hosted by President Barack Obama and First Lady Michelle Obama. David Jones, President of the State Troopers Fraternal Association Union, took offense to the lyrics in Common's track 'A Song for Assata.' 'A Song for Assata' pays homage to Joanne Chesimard, aka Assata Shakur, who was convicted of killing a New Jersey Police officer during a controversial trial in 1973. Shakur escaped prison in 1979 and is currently residing in Cuba under political asylum, although the United States Government is still offering a $1 million dollar reward for her capture. The State Troopers Fraternal Association Union is upset because Common's visit comes as they prepare to head to Washington, D.C., to honor slain officers at the National Law Enforcement Memorial.

Dr. Angela Davis

An American revolutionary Marxist Feminist political activist, philosopher, academic, and author who currently serves as a professor at the University of California, Santa Cruz, once posed a thought-provoking question:

"The idea of freedom is inspiring. But what does it mean? If you are free in a political sense but have no food, what's that? The freedom to starve?"

This statement highlights the importance of not only political freedom but also the necessity for basic needs such as food to truly experience and fully enjoy that freedom.

Introduction

This is the first series of my book that reflects on my future as a human rights activist. Using my life experiences as a multiracial woman, understanding and facing the challenges of racism and sexism, along with my own struggle with colorism, I will be writing this series in reverse. And this results in the future being the past.

I will first touch upon my struggles and challenges as a soldier, that being a soldier is beyond my uniform, emphasizing the encounters of activism, the future of police accountability, and racial equality, along with the rights of victims. I will discuss my personal struggles with understanding the activism process, the rules, the barriers, and the reason why artificial intelligence will take police accountability to a level of more controversy than in previous years. This includes trust factors of citizens with the police and how it feels being a mother with children who must walk around being looked at as black and not human.

How can we build relationships with the AI police? How do we continue activism if no fight is needed? How do I look to people who I serve if I want to quit? How will my work be remembered?

These questions will probably never be answered. Let's see how many of the answers I will get. Thank you for joining me. Please continue to read me. And you can always, always reach out to me at www.kathygreggs.com.

Acknowledgment

The most profound gratitude I wish to express is directed towards my mentor and guide, **The Lord Jesus Christ** Himself. The presence of His wisdom and love has been a constant source of motivation and inspiration, propelling me forward even in the face of challenges, even at the times I doubted myself. His guidance has taught me invaluable lessons, allowing me to navigate the intricacies of this journey with confidence and grace.

The following individuals and organizations deserve my utmost gratitude:

My Children: Thank you for your unwavering support in my work for the community and the people.

My Mother and Father: I am grateful to have parents like you who have accepted and supported me through all stages and transitions of my life.

My Sister: Your love, support, and trust mean more to me than words can express.

My Brother: Thank you for being an anchor in my life. Your love, support, and trust are invaluable.

R.L Smith: You are my world, the love of my life, the sun in my morning, the moon of my night. I could never have done this without you.

My best friend Shuntel Hines: Thank you for always pushing me to be my best. Your contribution to my book is greatly appreciated.

Former Senator Kirk DeViere: Your mentorship has been a significant blessing in my life. I aspire to become what I want because of your guidance.

Brother Benard Brooks: Thank you for your encouragement in helping me reach my goals.

Mario Hardy, DCW2: Thank you for your support and encouragement throughout my life and organization.

Raymond Johnson and Herman Hodges: Thank you both for your donations and encouragement in my life and this book.

Michael Sheehan: I am grateful for your motivation in helping me achieve my dream.

Karla Icaza: Thank you for investing your faith in me and inspiring me to participate in the community as a volunteer.

Sharon Campbell, Sharon Campbell Solution: Thank you for believing in me and motivating me to accomplish all of this.

Rev. Dr. Floyd Wicker: Thank you for always correcting me and motivating me to follow the right path.

Dr. Crystal Matthews: I will be eternally grateful for the support you provided when I needed it the most.

Michelle Jemmott: Thank you for being there for me. Friends like you come along once in a lifetime, and the world needs more.

Carrie Jackson, Subtle Touch Marketing: Thank you for being a great manager for my book.

Lemoi Desina, ASTP Photography: Thank you for assisting me with photography in this book and for your support throughout the years of my activism.

Veronica Jones, CEO of JonesGlobal Foundation, and Judy Buchmiller, member of Fayetteville NOW Chapter: You are both blessings from God. I cannot thank you enough for being there for me.

Paul Taylor: The assistance you have provided me on multiple occasions has been invaluable.

Shaun McMillian, Co-Founder Fayetteville PACT: I wanted to express my sincere appreciation for your consistent support and assistance. Your willingness to help and attention to detail have made a significant difference in my work. Thank you for being a reliable colleague.

Bernard Robinson (Mossburg): Your support has been a source of inspiration to me. Thank you for believing in me and pushing me to reach new heights. I'm grateful to have such an amazing friend like you.

Dr. Kimberly Muktarian, Save our Sons Raleigh: Thank you for always being there to offer a helping hand. Your reliability and generosity have not gone unnoticed, and I appreciate your continued support.

Monique Edwards, Board member of Fayetteville PACT: I wanted to extend my deepest gratitude for your consistent support and encouragement. Your belief in my abilities has boosted my confidence and allowed me to achieve more than I thought possible. Thank you for being an amazing colleague.

Chilkeo Hurst, Board member of Fayetteville PACT: Thank you for your exceptional support and dedication. Your expertise and guidance have been invaluable, and I'm grateful to have you as a colleague.

James Thomas, Board member of Fayetteville PACT: Thank you for being a constant source of positivity and optimism. Your enthusiasm and energy have made our work environment vibrant and enjoyable. I appreciate your presence as a colleague.

Jerome Bell, Board member of Fayetteville PACT: I am deeply thankful for your unwavering support and encouragement. Your positivity and enthusiasm have made our workplace a more vibrant and enjoyable environment. Thank you for being a remarkable colleague.

Devonta Banks, Board member of Fayetteville PACT: I wanted to thank you for being such a reliable and dependable colleague. Your support, especially during high-pressure situations, has helped me navigate challenges with ease. I'm grateful to have you on my team.

Pastor Anthony Faison, Board member of Fayetteville PACT: Thank you for being more than a colleague. Your friendship and unwavering support have made a significant impact on my life. I'm fortunate to have you as a favorite colleague.

Laura Hardy, Hardy Group LLC: I appreciate your dedication and the valuable contributions you bring to the team. Your skills and expertise are invaluable, and we're fortunate to have you as a colleague.

Gloria De Santos: Thank you for being more than a colleague. Your friendship and unwavering support have made a significant impact on my life. I'm fortunate to have you as a favorite colleague.

Former Council Member Christopher Davis: Words cannot adequately express my gratitude for your consistent support. Your patience and understanding during challenging times have been a source of strength for me. Thank you for being an amazing colleague.

Dr. Felicia Arriaga, NCSPAN: Thank you for being my sounding board and offering valuable insights. Your perspective and input have helped me make better decisions. I appreciate your guidance and support as a colleague.

Tamika Blu, NCBLOC Leader: I wanted to express my sincere gratitude for the tremendous support you've provided. Your willingness to step in and help out when needed has made a significant difference in my work, and I'm truly thankful.

Pam Wade, Member of Fayetteville Chapter NOW: I'm truly grateful for your unwavering support. Your belief in my abilities and your encouragement have motivated me to push through challenges and achieve success.

Treavor Flannery and Andy Shoenig, MDC Rural Forward: Thank you both for being exceptional collaborators and partners in our projects. Your teamwork and dedication have contributed to our success. I'm grateful to have you as colleagues.

SFC (R) Lammoth Oneal: Thank you for being there for me through this trial in my life. Few people can say they have such an understanding colleague/boss. I feel very lucky and grateful.

Cynthia Hale, CEO of National Domestic Violence Rally: I feel incredibly fortunate to have you as a colleague and friend. Your support and kindness.

SFC (R) Todd Henderson and Thomas Rice: Thank you both for being there for me. Friends like you come along once in a lifetime, and the world needs more.

Tiffany Logan: I wanted to extend my heartfelt thanks for your consistent support. Your encouragement and assistance have boosted my confidence and made me feel valued as a friend.

Gary Jones, Get with the Program: Thank you for being a constant pillar of support in my professional life. Your words of encouragement and your ability to lift my spirits have been instrumental in helping me stay motivated and focused. I truly appreciate your presence.

Conrad Simms, Military Brats: Your encouragement and belief in me have helped me overcome obstacles and achieve my goals.

Bilbo Stroud: You have been there for me throughout my entire life whenever I needed you. Thank you for always supporting my hopes, goals, and dreams.

Jackie Elliott: Thank you for being my go-to person whenever I needed help. Your expertise and willingness to share your knowledge have been invaluable, and I truly appreciate it.

Rhonda Shirley, Member of Fayetteville PACT: Thank you for being there for me. "Happiness is having a coworker who becomes a friend." I'm grateful for our friendship.

SGM (R) Aubrey Bradley: I wanted to extend my heartfelt thanks for your consistent support. Your encouragement and assistance have boosted my confidence and made me feel valued as a friend.

Natasha Crumbles-Mitchell, Military Brats: Your encouragement and belief in me have helped me overcome obstacles and achieve my goals.

Brooklyn Nelson: I wanted to extend my heartfelt thanks for your consistent support. Your encouragement and assistance have boosted my confidence and made me feel valued as a friend.

Stacie Borrello: I wanted to express my deep appreciation for your continuous support and belief in me. Your confidence in my abilities has inspired me to strive for excellence. Thank you!

Dr. Tina Barr, Former Vice President Fayetteville PACT: I am truly grateful for your consistent support and teamwork. Your collaborative spirit and willingness to lend a hand have made our projects smoother and more successful. Thank you for being an exceptional colleague.

MSG(R) Yvette Bell: I am so grateful for your support and mentorship. Thank you for everything you've taught me throughout my career. You played a large role in shaping me into the leader I am today.

Chermalatta Brown, CEO of Butterflies and Pearls: I wanted to extend my deepest appreciation for your consistent support. Your dedication and willingness to help have been an inspiration to me. Thank you for being an exceptional colleague and an invaluable part of our team.

Minster Amon Muhammad, #34 Mosque Durham: Thank you for being a constant pillar of support in my professional life. Your words of encouragement and your ability to lift my spirits have been instrumental in helping me stay motivated and focused. I truly appreciate your presence.

Brother Richard Muhammad: I am so grateful for your unwavering support throughout our journey together. Your dedication and encouragement have truly made a difference in my professional growth.

Jamal Johnson, SKU Philadelphia: I wanted to take a moment to thank you for your consistent support during challenging times. Your positivity and encouragement have helped me stay motivated and focused. Thank you!

Dr. Rev Curtis Gatewood: I am so grateful for your unwavering support throughout our journey together. Your dedication and encouragement have truly made a difference in my professional growth.

Fayetteville PACT Volunteers: Thank you to all of our volunteers! We can't do this without you!

Bishop Brian Thompson: I actually personally believe that no other person could ever be a better pastor than you in this entire world.

SGM (R) Louis Dillon: Thank you for making me achieve my dreams and become a better person in society. I am grateful to have you as my mentor.

SGM(R) William Griffin: Thank you for offering your continuous support and bringing out the best work of my career.

Rachel Battle: I am grateful for your help and support.

Kentavious Cooper: Your support and assistance means so much to me.

MSG Ramirez: Your contribution and assistance mean so much to me.

SGM (R) Ricky Gaines: Thank you for your guidance throughout my career. You motivated me when challenges arose and gave me the encouragement I needed.

MAJ (R) Eric Olson: Thank you for being an inspiring mentor and helping me unlock my potential.

SFC (R) Brandon Harris: Thank you for making my ideas feel valued and encouraging me to step outside the box and get creative.

SFC(R) Michael Stennis: I appreciate your support, help, mentorship, and constant support.

SFC (R) Eric Swallick: Thank you to an outstanding mentor and friend. I appreciate all of the lessons you've shared and the advice you've given me.

MAJ (R) Fayetteville Police Department James Nolette: Thank you for teaching me what it means to be a leader who guides others instead of directs them. I've taken all of the advice you've given me throughout my career and finally feel like I've become a great leader.

NC National Organization for Women President Gailya Paliga: Thank you for always encouraging me to put my best foot forward. No matter what situation arises.

City of Fayetteville Mayor Mitch Colvin: Thank you for teaching me what it means to be a leader who guides others instead of directs them.

City of Fayetteville Mayor (2013-2017) Nat Robertson: I want to let you know that your hard work and determination don't go unnoticed.

Maria Miller (R) LTC: I appreciate your dedication and the valuable contributions you bring to the team.

Alpha Elispon Chapter (Raliegh) Eta Phi Beta: You all have touched my life in a special way, and I will forever be thankful for how my life has changed since I met you all.

Brother Polymin Muhammad: I appreciate your dedication and valuable contributions.

Calli McMullen: I appreciate your dedication and valuable contributions.

Lawrence Carroll: I appreciate your dedication and valuable contributions.

Derrick Ward: I appreciate your dedication and valuable contributions.

About the Author

During the Uprising of the George Floyd Movement, Kathy Greggs, MBA of Human Resource Management, Co-Founder of Fayetteville Police Accountability Community Taskforce was in the spotlight on Police Reform. Kathy Greggs worked to build relationships with other Activists across the United States and International. Many didn't agree with her tactics and looked at her as she was still in the US ARMY. She decided to make a Movie to show the importance of capitalism and systematic racism on Amazon Prime "Fayetteville PACT American Rescue Plan" 2022, unscripted and unedited. She worked outside of her organization as an advocate because her scars were not her own.

Her book is written in reverse starting with how the future of activists looks. Will she stop, because of Artificial

Intelligence? Kathy Greggs grew up in Military home in Germany, she came to the United States to see what racism, sexism and colorism looked like.

Let's read her current journey along with her future path.

Contents

Dedication I
Introduction XV
Acknowledgment XVII
About The Author XXVII
Chapter 1: Activism Vs. Advocacy 30
Chapter 2: Artificial Intelligence For Police 37
Chapter 3: The Struggles Within 58
Chapter 4: Today And Tomorrow 85
Chapter 5: The Mother, The Soldier, And The Activist "The Way Ahead" 132

Page left Blank Intentionally

Chapter 1: Activism vs. Advocacy

First and foremost, I would like to provide a definition of what advocacy is. The Webster's dictionary clearly states: *"The act or process of supporting a cause or proposal: the act Or process of advocating (see ADVOCATE entry 2) something."*[2]

Activism, on the other hand, has a different meaning. Webster's dictionary defines it as "A doctrine or practice that emphasizes direct vigorous action, especially in support of or opposition to one side of a controversial issue." (Merriam-Webster. (n.d.). *Activism definition & meaning*. Merriam-Webster.

https://www.merriam-webster.com/dictionary/activism). The reason I wanted to highlight the differences in their definitions is

---

[2] (Merriam-Webster. (n.d.). Advocacy definition & meaning.

Merriam-Webster. https://www.merriam-webster.com/dictionary/advocacy). That is advocacy.

because, as an activist, I first started off doing *advocacy* to understand the difference of what I was advocating for.

Many people try to push the idea that activists are better than advocates. Looking at it differently from activist groups, they have people who are just citizens who come out to show support for the cause and reason for support. Most groups have diverse organization leaders, and the majority of those leaders for activism are of color and women. There are also people who are in the organization for activists who understand the cause because they may have themselves faced injustices or social injustices. After having a non-profit for eight years, I believe that the goal of the non-profit is for activism and advocacy to go hand in hand.

Eventually, as human beings with artificial intelligence, we must make sure that we understand that the movement is not just for one but for all people. All people must realize that with all honesty, transparency, and accountability from government officials and agencies – How do we get this? How many lives must be sacrificed to get it? Who are the important passive government officials? Who are the allies? Who will give us the most barriers? Who will not listen? Many questions, but none answered. We will need to understand the system and the people who govern it before we can negotiate, or even bargain, for any type of social justice. Fayetteville PACT will develop a team to get a resolution based on policy and dismantling of the Constitution and the 13th, 14th, and 15th amendments. These are the most powerful amendments that assist with systematic racism in the criminal justice system. I don't like to use the word "reform" because reforming is something that was never built for people and won't be accomplished.

Dismantling the system — yes, that can be rebuilt based on the people who seek democracy. Fayetteville PACT only plays one part on the chessboard. We need more people and more activists to come along and fight this. It takes more voices and more people, and unfortunately, sometimes even death. We must not fail, be the voice for the unheard, and be willing to die for victory. Not saying just words but also showing that we must win for the democracy of humanity. How does humanity exist if we're arguing with other activist groups?

As you see, in the media, Black Lives Matter was an influential activism group across the US and Internationally during and for the Trevor Martin and the Michael Brown movement. They rose even higher during the George Floyd movement. The Black Lives Matter movement has always existed alongside the Civil Rights Movement.

However, that group itself came under scrutiny for embezzlement, misappropriation of funds, and utilizing Black spaces for manipulation to receive funds from groups or foundations that were associated with white supremacy or confederacy. According to a CNN article, Shalomyah Bowers, an executive of Black Lives Matter (BLM), has been accused of diverting $10 million from BLM donors. The accusation is mentioned in a lawsuit. [3] The Washington Examiner also

---

[3] "Black Lives Matter executive Shalomyah Bowers accused of 'syphoning' $10M from BLM donors, suit says" by CNN. Available at:

published an article questioning whether BLM prioritizes black lives or white money.[4]

We also have a lot of activists around the world who have advocated for many years, including at the international level – we must all come together in the fight for humanity because humanity cannot exist without advocacy or activism.

Advocacy is something that is immensely important to me because when I first started Fayetteville PACT and my advocacy, it took a lot from me to even go into some of these areas. One area was, of course, advertising for survivors. And what I mean by advertising is assisting survivors in telling their stories and providing them with an open space to do so. This was especially hard for me because I am a survivor, but you'll see that when you read the next series. Right now, we're talking about advocacy. Advocacy is a lot of work. Advocacy could take over 10-20 years before any change or justice is implemented.

Doctor Reverend Martin Luther King's dream remains relevant to this date. To have a nation free from racism, where people could live in harmony without being judged by the color of their skin.

---

https://www.cnn.com/2022/09/04/us/black-lives-matter-executive-lawsuit

/index.html

[4] "Does BLM care about black lives or white money?" by Washington Examiner. Available at: https://www.washingtonexaminer.com/restoring-america/equality-not-eliti sm/does-blm-care-about-black-lives-or-white-money

"I have a dream that my four little children will one day live in a nation where they will not be judged by the color of their skin but by their character."[5]

While much social progress has been made, there is still much work to be done. It takes many years of study, research, and gaining trust. When you are welcomed into those rooms to advocate for a victim or even to advocate for yourself or someone you may know, you must make sure that you have empathy, sympathy, and compassion. Only those stories that the advocate is telling can be voiced. Your own opinion can contradict the cause or even the outcomes.

Most officials want to hear the true stories of the individual who has the most impact. How do we change the narrative to assist a client or a victim when we go into the room? Well, we must leave behind all our personal agendas. We must go into it making sure that we have a clear understanding that this could be you. This could be your friend, this could be your son, this could be your cousin, your brother, your sister, or your Grandma. With that, they would then see that you have the same compassion that the individual survivor may have had and lost. Giving hope and finding freedom is what we need to do, not only as advocates but as activists as well.

---

[5] [The Embassy of the United States in the Republic of Korea. (n.d.). Martin

Luther King Jr.'s "I Have a Dream" Speech (1963). Retrieved

from](https://kr.usembassy.gov/martin-luther-king-jr-dream-speech-1963/ #:~:text=I have a dream that my four little children will, I have a dream today)

Will activists still exist with AI? Will AI take over the compassion that human beings have for each other? Will AI understand the empathy that is needed to even have a mutual ground with human beings? That is something that we must look forward to as we move into the future. Are our kids doomed because we have AIs vs. advocates standing in the room? Are our kids doomed if we have no activists around? These are questions.

However, we have so many activist groups and organizations doing the same advocacy work that it becomes a source of confusion for the people we serve. In this case, who should we trust? Who should we be transparent with? What groups do we go for, and what groups do we not go for? These are the questions that we, as Fayetteville PACT, ask people on the streets, people that we don't know, strangers that follow us. How do you see us?

Do you see us as a group that is fulfilling our duty as activists? Or should we no longer advocate? Do you think that we can continue this in the future? Or do you think that we should not? What is your take on it? How do you see the advocacy that you may have? How do you see yourself going out to fight for a cause that you have never ever been impacted by?

How can you trust the activists if they're not there for you? We have activist groups, as well as attorneys, that come in when there is injustice, take photos for clout, and leave the family in their time of need without getting them justice.

They never come back to assist those families or individual victims in gaining justice. These so-called 'activists' come out when there is a spotlight when they can be on a podium, and then they exit themselves and never go back and show support, such as giving them money for groceries and assisting them with medical or mental health counseling. We must all come together in the fight for humanity because humanity cannot exist without advocacy or activism. So many people love to call themselves activists but are not really activists. It is hard to define and look for advocates and activists when we have people who are not real activists.

How can we expect people to trust us if they think we will leave and never help them find real justice? That is a question we should all think about.

Chapter 2: Artificial Intelligence For Police

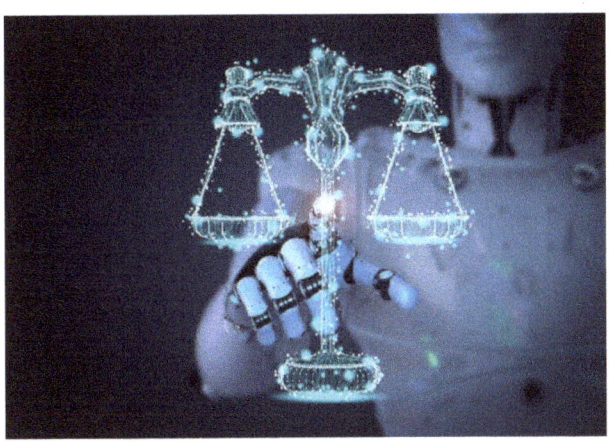

How does Artificial Intelligence work with Human Police Officers? Who is controlling the AI police? Who are the oversights of the AI police? These are questions that need to be answered. The future of activists and advocacy at risk.

After conducting a thorough analysis of several movies centered around police accountability, such as Minority Report, RoboCop, and The Creator, I was struck by the potential implications of artificial intelligence on the criminal justice system. These films served as a reminder of how AI may replace human empathy and sympathy in addressing instances of injustice and crime in the future. The implications of such a shift in power and responsibility are immense and require careful consideration.

The movie Minority Report offers a thought-provoking glimpse into the potential role of artificial intelligence in predicting and preventing crime. The futuristic setting of the movie, set in the year 2054, the film portrays a future where police use advanced technology to predict murders before they happen. However, it is important to note that the technology only predicts murders and no other crimes such as sexual assault, robbery, or suicide. [6]

In Minority Report, the limitations of relying solely on science to dictate justice are exposed. The concept of pre-crime is introduced, demonstrating how it can be used to deter crime and reduce criminal activity in communities. This approach also raises ethical concerns about the potential for false accusations and the impact on civil liberties.

As we look toward the future, it is worth considering how this technology may evolve and impact law enforcement practices nationwide. Will it lead to a safer society, or will it be misused and abused? Only time will tell, but it is important to carefully consider the potential benefits and drawbacks of relying on artificial intelligence in the criminal justice system.

This movie came out in 2002, in June, and during this time, we had several different researchers determine when artificial intelligence will take over. As the world recovered from the infamous Y2K scare, a new fear took hold: the possibility of computers seizing control, leading to the extinction of mankind. Comparisons were drawn to the demise of ancient creatures like dinosaurs and apes, but with a significant twist – unlike these

---

[6] Roger Ebert. (n.d.). Minority Report movie review & film summary.

Retrieved from https://www.rogerebert.com/reviews/minority-report-2002

natural wonders, AI is a creation of human hands. This raises a question: are we on the brink of being replaced by our own inventions, or are these fears mere figments of our imagination?

Suddenly, a plethora of questions and fears arose in people's minds. The very existence of humans was called into question as the rise of artificial intelligence loomed over them. Will humans still have a place in this world if they are replaced by machines? Will they get a fair trial if they are accused of a crime and artificial intelligence takes over in the police departments?

The thought of manipulation in the systems we have set up sent shivers down many people's spines. What if artificial intelligence gets involved in facial recognition or surveillance? Will it be manipulated to serve certain interests? The fear of racial profiling and police accountability not being followed anymore was too much to bear.

The thought of artificial intelligence becoming the judge and jury in the criminal justice system was enough to send chills through peoples' spines. Will we see a future where the robot is always right, and the human is always wrong? Will this stop the need for qualified immunity for police officers? Will this stop racial discrimination in the criminal justice system? The fear of mass incarceration in jails was too much to bear.

Though these systems have already been set up for us to continue to fight and to have oversight, how do we have oversight over artificial intelligence? Who is running the artificial intelligence Police Department? The thought of job loss due to artificial intelligence taking over not only the police departments but also in areas of administration jobs, food jobs, manufacturing jobs, and industrial jobs was too much to bear. The chaos and emotions that people were feeling were palpable.

Although we may not have all the answers, it's worth discussing what the future holds for activism and advocacy, both in the streets and behind a computer desk. Can we use technology to advocate for injustices we witness? Will it help us bring justice to families who have waited too long? And can technology play a larger role in reviewing police accountability or racial profiling lawsuits in cities and counties? These are important questions that we should consider as we navigate the future of activism. Since 2016, the Fayetteville PACT has been advocating for the establishment of a civilian police oversight authority that includes Citizen Review Boards. Their efforts have been focused on ensuring greater accountability and transparency in law enforcement, which is a crucial step towards building trust between the community and the police force.

The Fayetteville PACT strongly believes that having an attorney and two private investigators with administrative data personnel, who are entirely independent of the City Council and the AI-powered Police Department, can serve as a single partitioner. This team will investigate cases related to police profiling, racial disparities, and police accountability, with citizens having their own board to review all evidence, including video footage, statements, and the officer's record. This board will be able to assess if any police accountability issues have occurred in the past.

In a time when police accountability is at the forefront of public discourse, this system has been developed to provide transparency and oversight. It aims to make the process seamless and more efficient for the citizens. This system works towards ensuring that justice is served without the burden of legal fees falling on the shoulders of citizens seeking recourse for police officers who may have violated their constitutional or civil rights. It's no secret that money plays a significant role in the criminal justice system, including police accountability. Unfortunately, many people are unaware of the budget and spending of their local police departments. However, several organizations have been working to address this issue, including the Budget and Tax Center in North Carolina. Additionally, a collective North Carolina statewide police accountability network, led by black leaders, has been established to provide policy training and understanding at the local level.

During these trainings, participants were introduced to the concept of reallocating funds from police department budgets to areas in need. This raises the question: what role will artificial intelligence (AI) play in budgeting for police departments? How much will it cost to implement AI technology in the department, and how will it affect the job of police officers?

Research has been conducted on AI pilot programs aimed at testing the effectiveness of AI police officers compared to their human counterparts. These programs provide insight into the potential benefits and drawbacks of implementing AI technology in police departments. As this technology continues to evolve, it's crucial to carefully consider the implications and ensure that any changes made prioritize public safety and accountability.

One of the first studies that I reviewed, and which caught my attention was on 'The use of advanced technology in law enforcement,' which is a fascinating topic, and a recent study showcased a pilot program in New York that implemented innovative RoboCops to patrol the subway system. The K5 robot, created by Knightscope, was part of the program for two months, and the aim of this project is to bring more support to New York's police departments to aid officers in their fight against crime.[7]

It's interesting to note that the technology behind the RoboCops is from NVID. The K54 robots in New York use this technology, which was developed by Knightscope and is powered by the AI supercomputer Jetson, named after the famous cartoon from the 1960s. The AI platform assists police officers during arrests and can even identify criminal actions or individuals. However, it's important to note that this system is designed to provide additional support to officers, not replace them.

It will certainly be interesting to see if this technology proves successful in New York's pilot program and if it will be implemented across the whole United States. The use of advanced AI-powered support like this could potentially change the future of law enforcement as we know it, bringing more safety and security to our communities. The future will certainly look very different from today.

---

[7] [8] RoboCop Returns - Will It Ever Happen? (n.d.). Retrieved from https://www.looper.com/176713/robocop-returns-release-date-plot-and-c ast/

In 2017, CNN Business published an article discussing the possibility of implementing remote-controlled law and order. The article highlighted how Dubai Police was planning to test these waters by introducing a fleet of robots in their ranks. While this may not be Skynet, the plan is to recruit enough robots to make up 25% of the police department by 2030. This move raises several questions, of course. While it may seem like a PR stunt or something straight out of the movie RoboCop, the laws governing the use of robots are very real. As per the movie, a RoboCop may not injure a human being, and it must obey orders given to it by human beings, except when such orders conflict with the first law.

In Dubai, these 75-year-old laws provide an outline for the creation of robotics, which are called robots. The name itself is derived from the movie RoboCop. The first robot was unveiled in 2011 by Powell Robots of Spain. And weighed 220 pounds and stood five feet six inches tall.

The two-arm wheelbase service robots could speak nine languages out of the box. These robots were highly customizable by their creators to suit different needs. The designer envisioned these robots to be interactive service providers for people. This was in 2011 when robot cops were initiated in Dubai, which is called robocops.

Brigadier Collide Macarius Island, the general director of the Smart Services Department at the police, was responsible for the entire police robot project. He stated that the robots were designed to be an interactive service for people. With their language capabilities and customizable features, these robots could provide a range of services to people, making them an innovative addition to the city's police force. The introduction of these robots was a significant milestone in the development of robotics and AI-powered technologies. It was a step towards creating a safer and more efficient society where technology could be leveraged to provide better services to people.

It remains to be seen how successful the implementation of robots in law enforcement will be. However, it is clear that the move towards automation and the use of AI-powered technology is gaining traction across various industries. Only time will tell if this is the beginning of a new era in law enforcement or just another fleeting experiment. A lot of studies have been conducted on the use of artificial intelligence (AI) in law enforcement (police). Are the robots more human or less human than the actual police officers? That is the stage that we must understand and try to see throughout the process of the pilot program, not only in New York but other places. When it comes to RoboCop, what are the malfunctions that we may see in these robocops? Who keeps the data on these malfunctions? In the movie minority report, the data was breached, and the data was manipulated. Is there going to be manipulation of the data from the robocops? It's so many questions when it comes to artificial intelligence.

Well, let's move on to discussing the movie The Creator 2023. It's important to acknowledge that AI is an inevitable part of our evolution as a society. We cannot stop it from existing in the US or anywhere else in the world. However, as activists, we need to think about how we can navigate the use of artificial intelligence in policing.

As someone who has been an activist and an advocate for police accountability for over nine years at both local and global levels, I find it challenging to accept that we can entirely avoid the use of technology in policing. While we may not trust human police officers, it's difficult to put our faith in AI systems when it comes to policing.

In The Creator 2023, we see that even though artificial intelligence continues to advance and progress, there is still a lack of trust in the system. Most families do not trust human police officers, and it's uncertain how they would react to AI-powered policing. The movie shows us how robots and half-human robots must unite and fight against not only the police but also the United States Army. It's a thought-provoking movie that raises important questions about the role of AI in society.

In the movie, the robotic people and the police had to unite against the United States Army. The Army didn't approve of half-human, half-robotic individuals. They believed that humans should be the only creators and that no one should exist as half-human, half-robot. The movie's artificial intelligence police understood every individual's language in each city, and they took orders from a half-man, half-police officer called a "stunning." They followed orders without deviation unless instructed otherwise by their respective students.

I found this movie interesting because it depicted a scenario where AI and half-robot, half-human beings could work together because of their shared connection as robotics. The human beings, represented by the United States Army, fought against and attempted to eliminate the half-robot, half-humans. However, with the advent of new technology and the evolution of society, we cannot stop, turn around, or go backward in the evolutionary process. When we look into the pay of AI, and we look into the pay of a police officer, the comparison is just so interesting, and not only that, but it's also unavoidable. The cost of a police AI is $75,000, with cameras for one AI and sensors attached to their body for $75,000.

Now, when we're looking at the cost, let's look at how much it costs to maintain it. It says as little as $9840 a month to maintain and purchase the microrobot in 2012, as high as 267,955 for robots the size of riding a lawn mower that was in 2012. So, using these robots 24/7 and using maintenance on them could cost one individual Police Department over $5 million a year. This does not include the dog robots. The average police officer salary in the city of Fayetteville after graduation is $43,860 per year depending on experience level because they could go up to 65,790 per year depending on the police level.

Across the nation, lawsuits against police departments continue to soar, with some reaching a staggering $130 million. Police accountability, misconduct, and racial profiling are just a few of the issues that have resulted in such lawsuits. One of the most significant concerns regarding the justice system is the potential for false imprisonment and wrongful convictions. However, with the integration of AI-powered police, we can minimize the chances of such incidents occurring. Even though it may require a considerable investment, the cost of maintaining AI Police would still be more cost-effective if we compare it to the money utilized for lawsuits. This could potentially save both time and resources that could be utilized in other areas of the justice system by ensuring public safety and reducing the risk of human error.

The danger of using a human being as a police officer is higher than that of using an AI-powered cop. Police officers face a range of risks, including inadequate training, overtraining, egotism, and narcissism. While most police officers abide by policy, there are those who prefer to take matters into their own hands, leading to federal, city, and county lawsuits.

To be an effective police officer, one must be both physically and mentally fit. Mental fitness plays a huge role in police accountability, and this is where AI comes in. Due to financial hardships and mental illness, most police officers quit within their first five years and the ones that stay on face significant mental health challenges. Post-traumatic stress disorder and suicidal tendencies are common among police officers, and they are not receiving proper treatment.

While we now have AI-powered police officers, we need to acknowledge that AI officers working with mentally unstable human beings can also lead to chaos. The question arises: Will activists protest against the use of artificial intelligence in policing? Will human police officers unite with activists against AI police?

We must address these issues to ensure that our police officers can serve the public effectively and safely. The key is to train and evaluate police officers correctly while providing them with the resources they need to maintain their mental health. We also need to find a way to use AI-powered police officers while ensuring that they work together with human police officers to serve and protect the public.

Many activists view police officers as inferior, while some police officers may view the public as a threat. Who should be feared more?

As society looks to the future, the role of artificial intelligence in policing is an increasingly pressing concern. While police officers are supposed to be public servants, protecting and serving the people, questions arise regarding how AI-powered officers will be trained and ultimately deployed. Will they be programmed to treat all individuals, regardless of race, with the same level of respect and dignity that human officers are expected to provide?

These questions are particularly pertinent in light of longstanding concerns about racial disparities in policing. Activists have been fighting for years to address these disparities, and it is essential that any new technology introduced into the policing arena is subject to the same level of scrutiny and accountability.

At Fayetteville PACT, we believe in upholding these important values. We know that the impact of AI on policing is complex and multifaceted, and we are committed to ensuring that any new technology is implemented in a way that serves the public interest. As the world around us continues to evolve, it is more important than ever that we remain vigilant in our efforts to promote fairness and justice in all areas of society.

Our argument is oversight and who oversights the police. Race, gender, ethnicity, and religion have nothing to do with policing. We found by looking in different cities, counties, states, as well as national states, that police officers are not trained effectively and also not evaluated effectively to be public servants as well as career-driven police officers. Most police officers quit within five years of being a police officer due to financial hardships and mental illness.

Police officers become suicidal and suffer from post-traumatic stress disorder that is not being treated properly. Though we have AI police officers, we also need to make sure that we understand that AI police officers working with human beings that is mentally unstable can also cause chaos to those they serve.

Will activists be able to actually initiate some type of protest against artificial intelligence versus human beings? Will the activists and the human being police unite against the AI police? Advocacy and activism activists must come together in a form of understanding evolution as well as in a form of understanding community policing. As we look at many different neighborhoods in the city of Fayetteville, we never see community policing. How does community policing look in your neighborhood? Does community policing actually work? Well, the answers to these questions are based on who lives in what community and what community resources are offered.

The oversight of the police is a critical issue that we must address as a society. It is what our whole argument is based on. Regardless of race, gender, ethnicity, or religion, policing should be done effectively and fairly. However, our research across different cities, counties, states, and national states has revealed that police officers are not being trained or evaluated effectively to be both public servants and career-driven officers. Advocacy and activism must come together to understand the evolution of community policing. Unfortunately, many neighborhoods in the city of Fayetteville lack community policing. It's essential to recognize that community policing's effectiveness depends on the resources available in each community and who lives in them.

In many rural and urban communities, there exists a stark contrast in the availability of resources compared to suburban and predominantly white communities. This disparity is particularly evident in Latino and Native American communities, which often lack essential resources due to either their limited provision or complete absence. Resources encompass not only financial support but also community intervention programs and initiatives aimed at fostering economic development and growth within these communities.

An important question arises when considering the implementation of AI robot police: will they be able to uphold economic growth, or could they potentially hinder it? Will AI police impede the progress of infrastructure development? It is crucial to understand that community policing requires the active involvement of all members within a specific community. This involvement extends beyond assisting with interactions or responding to crimes; it also encompasses participating in the community's development and growth process. Unfortunately, trust, honesty, and transparency within our communities have eroded over time. Several factors contribute to this, including high crime rates, human trafficking, and a lack of effective policing. It is essential to acknowledge that even within

Fayetteville, NC, there are areas where policing is inconsistent and budgetary concerns are not adequately addressed.[8][9]

Police departments receive extensive funding, with budgets often exceeding $35 million per county. However, the overspending or underspending of these budgets significantly impacts the economic growth of communities in need. Although the Census Bureau system is employed to allocate resources, concerns have been raised regarding its manipulation and the accuracy of the data it provides.[10]

Questions regarding fraud, waste, and abuse arise. Are police departments guilty of engaging in such practices? How can we identify instances of fraud, waste, or mismanagement of funds? In Fayetteville, Pact has personally witnessed instances where

---

[8] [1] Katz v. United States: The Fourth Amendment adapts to new technology | Constitution Center. (n.d.). Retrieved from

https://constitutioncenter.org/blog/katz-v-united-states-the-fourth-amend ment-adapts-to-new-technology

[9] [2] ACLU. (2018, August 20). The NSA Continues to Violate Americans' Internet Privacy Rights. Retrieved from

https://www.aclu.org/news/national-security/nsa-continues-violate-ameri cans-internet-privacy

[10] [3] Bibology. (2018, December 18). Why JFK had to wiretap Martin Luther King. Retrieved from

https://www.washingtontimes.com/news/2019/jun/19/why-jfk-had-to-wir etap-martin-luther-king/

data presented to the City Council was manipulated or even nonexistent. Furthermore, there are several vehicles listed in the police department's budget that have never been used or have never been used.

Additionally, the training of police officers in riot tactics, particularly the practice of sending them to Israel at a cost exceeding $4 million annually, raises concerns. The militarization of communities, particularly those predominantly inhabited by Latino and Native American individuals, without sufficient resources perpetuates issues of police accountability and racial profiling. It begs the question: who polices the police?

While district attorneys are responsible for pressing charges against officers who violate constitutional and civil rights, Cumberland County and Fayetteville lack an effective system to fulfill this duty. As a result, individuals seeking justice for injustices perpetrated by the police department often resort to filing fedgEOI lawsuits due to the absence of an insurance policy that covers such cases. Most cities and counties have acquired insurance to cover police misconduct or brutality cases, often capping the coverage at $75,000 per case. While some officers face transfers or reprimands for misconduct, North Carolina statutes 160-1 and 160-8 explicitly prevent citizens from reviewing police officers' records or those of any government officials within the state. Access to personnel files requires a subpoena obtained through legal counsel, further limiting transparency and accountability.

Concerns regarding the utilization of AI police officers come to the forefront. Will the introduction of AI police reduce the number of lawsuits filed against the state? Will oversight of the police remain necessary? Can qualified immunity be applied to human police officers only?

These are critical questions that highlight the potential manipulation of power by the police, even without AI officers. The evolution of facial recognition, digital license plate detection, and surveillance technologies across cities, states, and even internationally has raised concerns among citizens regarding privacy infringement and the potential for criminalization.[11] While technology aids in life-saving preventive measures and enhances public safety, its cost-effectiveness and the extent to which taxpayers' money is required to sustain permanent AI policing programs remain under scrutiny. Policing efforts, including foot patrols, are evident across North Carolina, with police officers risking their lives daily. The introduction of AI police may help mitigate the loss of lives, including those of police officers. However, as human beings, it is crucial that we prioritize compassion and recognize the value of every individual in our communities.

Considering the potential implementation of AI police in North Carolina, it is worth exploring the outcomes of pilot programs conducted in New York. The continuous evolution of technology and society compels us to consider the implications

---

[11] [4] Napa Valley Register. (n.d.). Facial recognition technology: Man sues after arrest. Retrieved from https://napavalleyregister.com/news/nation-world/crime-courts/facial-rec ognition-technology-arrest-lawsuit-black-plaintiffs/article_b07958f0-8b0752e0-93a7-27c3eab7fe27.html

of AI police replacing human officers. While it may seem impossible to halt this evolutionary progression, activists must continue advocating for justice and ensuring that the utilization of AI in policing does not infringe upon individuals' rights.

The oversight of AI police, the need for civilian police oversight, and the potential impact on employment within police departments are critical aspects to be addressed.

This transition towards AI police also raises concerns about the economy. Will cities accumulate debt by prioritizing AI over human resources? Activists must grapple with negotiating with police departments to ensure responsible financial utilization of AI equipment. The deployment of AI police in predominantly black communities, such as Atlanta, New York, California, Louisiana, New Orleans, Houston, TX, and Florida, raises concerns about potential displacement and segregation based on race, religion, and gender. While there are numerous ways AI police could fail, activists continue to work towards eliminating AI and surveillance, advocating for privacy rights that protect individuals from constant monitoring.[12][13]

In the era of AI police, questions arise about what should be public and what should not. Concerns about potential racial bias and the criminalization of black and brown people loom large as

---

[12] [7] The Creator movie review & film summary. (n.d.). Retrieved from https://www.rogerebert.com/reviews/the-creator-movie-review-2023

[13] [5] PBS. (n.d.). AI on the battlefield. Retrieved from https://www.pbs.org/video/ai-on-the-battlefield-1688934485/

historical experiences with law enforcement raise doubts about the future implications of AI policing.

The lack of transparency regarding the utilization, equipment, software, and data storage within AI police systems only deepens these uncertainties. With the advent of AI police, one wonders how it will impact various aspects of society. Will it lead to widespread fear and reluctance to leave one's home due to pervasive facial recognition? Will individuals be hesitant to work in public sectors or jobs where AI police officers are employed for security? These are valid concerns as the full capabilities and implications of AI police remain unknown.[14]

Furthermore, the potential presence of AI police officers in prisons and schools raises further questions. Will AI police become a new authority figure within these institutions? How will AI police operate in malls, workplaces, and other public spaces? The consequences and implications of AI police officers being involved in crime prevention are complex and multifaceted.

As activists grapple with the evolution of AI police, they face internal struggles. Should they continue their fight or step back? Will quitting during this transformative period be seen as a failure? These are existential questions that activists must

---

[14] ACLU. (n.d.). Amazon's Face Recognition Falsely Matched 28 Members of Congress With Mugshots. Retrieved from

https://www.aclu.org/news/privacy-technology/amazons-face-recognitionfalsely-matched-28

confront while waiting for AI police programs to be implemented across cities and counties in the United States. The quest for justice remains paramount, even in the face of AI police. Unity within communities and a collective understanding of what AI police truly entail will be crucial. Safety is a fundamental right for everyone, and it is incumbent upon society to ensure that AI police systems do not perpetuate harm or discrimination.

Geoffrey Hinton, a renowned AI expert, offers insights into the capabilities and risks of artificial intelligence. [15] He acknowledges the significant potential of AI in areas such as healthcare and drug design but also highlights risks such as unintended biases and the misuse of AI systems. These concerns encompass fake news, employment bias, policing, and the use of battlefield robots.

At this critical juncture, it is essential to strike a balance between safety and the ethical implications of AI. As an activist, the fear of a ubiquitous AI police presence raises questions about the purpose and impact of their work.

It is a daunting era for all activists, advocates, and concerned individuals, prompting reflection on our readiness for such changes. Issues such as fake news, unintended bias in employment and policing, and the use of AI in warfare must be

---

[15] CBS News. (n.d.). Geoffrey Hinton on the promise, risks of artificial intelligence | 60 Minutes. Retrieved from

https://www.cbsnews.com/news/geoffrey-hinton-ai-dangers-60-minutes-tr anscript/

addressed. Public dialogue and rigorous assessment are necessary to determine the boundaries of public access to information and the safeguards needed to prevent abuse of power. As activists, we face a dilemma. Should we continue our work despite the evolution of AI police, or should we consider quitting? Will we be judged if we choose to step back during the installation of AI police programs across all cities and counties in the US?

What challenges will activists encounter as they strive to convince families to seek justice, even without unity with AI police? I firmly believe that justice will always prevail, but achieving it requires unity within communities and among all individuals worldwide. Everyone deserves safety, and ensuring it is a collective responsibility.

Chapter 3: The Struggles Within

Do you feel this book has fulfilled its purpose so far? Has it awakened the activist within you? Has it made you condemn the policies and the policymakers who divide us? Policymakers who will do anything for their own benefit.

Well, I really hope you are finding this book helpful somehow.

The lessons in this chapter are exceptionally enriching and invaluable, not only for their practical teachings but also for the inspiring philosophy they espouse. Beginning with a personal account of my own struggles as an activist, this series delves into the meaning of life in the face of death, encouraging us all to fight for what we believe in and live more fully. The second part reads like a gripping first-person narrative of the freedom struggle I lived through, a testament to the power of perseverance and courage in the face of injustice. To truly serve others, we must first cultivate humility, the essential foundation of servant leadership. But what does it mean to be humble, and why is it so important for public servants? As someone who has always recognized the needs of others, I know that genuine compassion is the driving force behind all acts of service.

Courage and a sense of responsibility are equally crucial traits for activists, who must always keep in mind that they are serving the public for the greater good. Our actions must be clear and accountable, always working towards the benefit of those we serve. As the Bible teaches us, a faithful servant is humble before God, ready to act on His directions, and inspired to meet the needs of others. Let us always remember our purpose as servants: to be a blessing to those around us.

It is not about money. It should never be about money. Yet, there are so-called activists out there who claim to be fighting for justice, but what they're really after is fame, fortune, and recognition. True public servants, on the other hand, don't need any of that. They serve out of a deep sense of compassion, empathy, and respect for something greater than themselves.

As a dedicated advocate for those who have been wronged or experienced injustice, I make it my mission to stand with my clients and their families. Whether it's fighting against police brutality and misconduct or seeking justice in other forms, my goal is to ensure that these individuals receive the support they need and the justice they deserve.

Unfortunately, the fight for justice is often an uphill battle, particularly when it comes to holding law enforcement accountable for their actions.

Qualified immunity can make it nearly impossible to seek justice for victims and their families, leaving them feeling helpless and frustrated.

Despite the challenges, however, I remain committed to helping families seek legal remedies and achieve the justice they deserve. Whether it's through monetary compensation or other means, I strive to ensure that families are treated with respect and dignity throughout the process.

Of course, not every family wants to go public with their case. Some prefer to settle things privately, without the glare of the media spotlight. As a public servant, it's important to respect these wishes and accommodate them as best I can.

At the end of the day, what matters most is that justice is served. As a compassionate and dedicated advocate, I will continue to fight for those who have been wronged and ensure that their voices are heard. We understand the gravity of the information we share with the public. That's why our team of experts is our most valuable asset. They ensure that every case is thoroughly reviewed and all evidence is analyzed before making any decisions. Whether we choose to proceed with the case or support the family member or next of kin in their pursuit of justice, we always hold ourselves accountable.

As an activist, I understand the risks that come with speaking out against injustice. But when I think about my children and the kind of world I want them to live in, I know that staying silent is not an option. Our mission at Fayetteville PACT is to fight for equitable justice for everyone, regardless of their background or circumstances.

Of course, our work is not without its challenges. Police accountability is a particularly sensitive issue, as it can often be seen as an attack on law enforcement as a whole. But we know that there are good people within the system who want to see positive change, and we're committed to working with them to make that happen.

At the end of the day, our goal is to empower families and communities to take control of their own destinies. We provide guidance and support throughout the legal process, but we also make sure that people understand their rights and options, even if they choose to go it alone. Criminal justice reform is just one piece of the puzzle; we also believe in building a strong, sustainable black infrastructure that can thrive without the influence of outside forces. It's not always easy, but we know that the work we're doing is important. By standing up for justice and speaking truth to power, we're helping to create a better, more equitable world for all of us.

In the heart of black and brown communities, the gaping void of resources and services poses a towering barrier to progress. I've gleaned insights from a dynamic training program orchestrated by the North Carolina Black Leaders Organized Collective, which painted a picture of unity - a single, supportive community.[16] Delving into the lives of luminaries like Doctor Huey Newton, Reverend Doctor Martin

---

[16] NC BLOC. (n.d.). Retrieved from https://www.ncbloc.black/

Luther King[17], Harriet Tubman, Sojourner Truth, and Fannie Mae Lou, I've chronicled our societal evolution, yet a troubling pattern emerges. Today, solidarity often remains confined within the boundaries of social groups or labels.

Our promise, however, is to bolster our community, vigilantly documenting any police misconduct. We are committed to shining a light on the hushed conversations around domestic violence, rape, incest, molestation, and drugs that lurk in the shadows of our neighborhoods. Born in Camden, NJ, raised in Germany, and a resident of Fayetteville, NC, since 2006, I've observed the dire economic plight of the black and brown populace, a situation crying out for immediate reform and an infusion of resources.

Caught in a dichotomy, I stand as a federal employee and a proud veteran, yet I am pained by the sight of veterans in our community left in the lurch. This includes homeless veterans, those reintegrating from Cumberland County detention center, and those wrongfully accused or convicted, their pleas for justice unheard.[18] Striving for justice and standing up for what's

---

[17] Britannica, T. Editors of Encyclopaedia. (2021, January 7). Martin Luther King, Jr. Encyclopedia Britannica.
https://www.britannica.com/biography/Martin-Luther-King-Jr

[18] Fayobserver. (2020, October 7). Voters' Guide: Cumberland County commissioners candidates. Fayobserver.
https://www.fayobserver.com/story/news/2020/10/07/voters-guide-cumb erland-county-commissioners-candidates/5881948002/

right, I'm disconcerted by the seeming lack of support in our collective struggle. The irony does not escape me that some who shy away from lending aid fill the pews on Sundays or extend their hands at organizations like the Salvation Army.

Even more intriguing is the reluctance of City Council members and county commissioners, who preside over a community teeming with people of color to address the injustices that tarnish their own city or county. The question that lingers is, how can we wage a battle for justice if those brave enough to stand against injustice are left to struggle in solitude? When it comes to seeking justice for strangers, it can be a delicate and challenging task. How do we persuade others to help when they have no personal connection to the cause? Is quoting scripture or questioning authority figures the best approach? These are the questions that arise when trying to rally support for the greater good. While some may find comfort in religious teachings, it may not be enough to sway those who are skeptical. The path to justice may be long and winding, but with the right approach, it's possible to bring about change for the better.

Here are a few suggestions:

- **Raise awareness:** Use various platforms such as social media, community events, or public meetings to share information about the injustices faced by those individuals. Educate people about the issue and explain why their support is crucial. Raise awareness about the injustice through social media channels using appropriate hashtags relevant to your cause. This can help garner attention from those who may be willing to support your cause.

- **Seek legal advice:** Consult with a lawyer or a legal aid organization specializing in the type of injustice you're dealing with. They can provide guidance on possible legal avenues and actions you can take.
- **Engage with community leaders:** Reach out to community leaders, including clergy members and pastors, expressing your concerns and seeking their guidance or involvement in addressing the issue at hand. They might have resources or connections that can help advance your cause.
- **Engage with community organizations:** Reach out to local community organizations that focus on social justice, human rights, or legal advocacy. They may have resources and networks dedicated to supporting those seeking justice.
- **Collaborate with advocacy groups:** Look for local organizations or groups that focus on social justice issues related to the problems you're trying to address. Join forces with them and work together towards a common goal.
- **Communicate with elected officials:** Contact your local government representatives who have taken an oath of office to serve the community as public servants. Share your concerns with them and request their assistance in advocating for justice on behalf of these individuals. Remember that building coalitions and fostering meaningful dialogue can make a significant impact when seeking justice for those who may not have a voice themselves.

Regarding religious institutions specifically, If you feel comfortable doing so, you can approach clergy members within your church community and share your concerns about the injustice affecting a member of their congregation. However, keep in mind that not all religious leaders may be directly involved in addressing societal injustices outside their faith community. It might also be worth exploring other churches or religious organizations known for their commitment to social justice causes if you feel they would be more receptive.

A vivid memory is etched in my mind. A meeting with two pastors, I won't be mentioning any names, for they may take offense. The topic of discussion was two instances of injustice. One pastor, quite bluntly, declared his congregation's inability to get involved despite the fact that the injustice involved a longstanding member of the church and his family. This pastor shared with me his personal belief in the police's actions of arresting and battering the individual I was representing. His reservations stemmed from his disapproval of the family's lifestyle and their actions within the community.

It was disheartening to hear a religious leader, expected to be a beacon of compassion and support, express such unequivocal bias. His support for the law enforcement's actions, without due consideration of all perspectives, was unsettling. Even more so was the fact that personal judgments about someone's lifestyle or actions were allowed to interfere with providing support in a time of crisis.

In the face of such resistance, I found myself questioning, was I in a place of worship or was I in a community where judgment was meted out freely? It was a stark reminder of how those who take the oath of office sometimes choose to selectively serve the public.

My pursuit of justice led me to the General Assembly, where I spoke to several representatives and senators about cases involving police misconduct, racial profiling, and wrongful arrest, not only in Cumberland County but also in other counties. One representative, in particular, was dismissive, stating his doubt about the progress of my endeavors due to his race and the race of the individual who had suffered the injustice.

These experiences have highlighted the hurdles that often stand in the way of justice. They've also underscored the importance of continuing to advocate for justice and equality despite the occasional dismissive official or unsupportive public servant. For every door that closes, another opens – in community organizations, advocacy groups, or civil rights and legal aid groups. These entities can guide us to navigate the system effectively.

If you still feel strongly about addressing these injustices within your community, it might be helpful to seek out other avenues of support, such as advocacy groups or organizations dedicated to social justice. These groups may provide resources and guidance on how best to address these issues in your specific context. Remember that not all individuals or institutions will share your viewpoint on certain matters.

However, change is gradual, and persistence is key. By continuing to voice concerns and seek support from various resources, we contribute to raising awareness and fostering societal change.

Probing the depths of public service, I often wonder how far a public servant should go. Would they risk their own livelihood to support someone seeking police accountability or justice against police misconduct? One name, however, offers a glimmer of hope amidst these questions – former Senator Kirk DeViere.[19]

Before his tenure as a senator, I knew DeViere as a city council member. A veteran and a business owner, DeViere was always about the community. Repeatedly, I've approached DeViere with cases of public interest or with clients he's never met. His response, irrespective of the hour, has always been one of steadfast support. From aiding domestic violence victims to securing more funds for the county, DeViere's commitment has been unflinching. DeViere and his wife have been regular attendees at protests, racial equality marches, workshops, and events in Fayetteville, Cumberland County, and Hope Mills. Notably, DeViere is a white man who has consistently assisted Fayetteville PACT and me, a domestic violence advocate. His unwavering dedication to the community underscores the importance of community policing and the role of public servants.

Regrettably, not all who run for office share DeViere's spirit. Some vie for power to fulfill personal agendas or to prop up their public image. They forget the attributes of leadership and public service - the need for compassion, the heart that compels us to provide hope. Why do some serve only their own race or

---

[19] deViere, K. (n.d.). A Note of Thanks. Kirk deViere. https://www.kirkdeviere.com/.

gender when we are all one race, one community? The path to unity and honor lies in helping each other, knowing or unknown.

Many cases I've come across have moved me to tears, making me question my pursuit of police accountability. Losses hit hard, leaving me to wonder what else could have been done. Yet, the struggle continues, driven by the quest for justice.

One case that left a profound impact was that of Timothy Smith, a young man suffering from mental illness. Smith had a job, a family, and a history. Following an incident involving his sister, a loaded gun, and a police officer, Smith was left bleeding on the ground while deputies walked past him. The sight of a young man crying out for help while bullets riddled his family's trailer left me in tears for hours.

While the authorities painted him as a felon who shot at a police officer, the truth stood starkly different. Smith had shot in the air, not at a police officer. The charges were an assault on a police officer and resisting arrest, which seemed unfathomable given Smith's condition post-shooting. The incident was a stark reminder of the inhumane acts that can be inflicted on individuals and the importance of continuing the fight for justice.

The Smith case served as a catalyst for a difficult conversation with my own children about law enforcement encounters. It underscored the need to distinguish between the law and excessive force and the importance of obeying the law, even when the force used seems excessive.[20]

As a public servant and an activist, the journey is fraught with difficult cases and hard questions. Yet, the fight for justice and accountability continues, fueled by the belief in a better, more equitable future. The role of a police officer extends beyond maintaining law and order. If an officer witnesses a colleague using excessive force and fails to intervene, they may be held liable for their inaction. This underscores the critical role they play in ensuring a safe and respectful work environment. However, a line exists between excessive force, which refers to more force than necessary in a given situation, and police brutality, which includes a range of misconduct, including excessive force. The latter often results in death, while the former may lead to injury or death.

These nuances led me to question the necessity of policing the police when I first started with Fayetteville PACT. Why must we continue to seek transparency, accountability, and responsibility from the police, the district attorney, and judges? Why must we ask them to adhere strictly to their policies, procedures, and the law? Amid these questions, I found myself reflecting on my military upbringing, where strict obedience and discipline were the norm.

---

[20] Legal Information Institute. (n.d.). Excessive force. Cornell Law School. https://www.law.cornell.edu/wex/excessive_force.

As an activist, I've found that not everyone shares the same perspectives. Some activists believe that all police officers are inherently bad, while others see all white people as racist or part of white supremacy. However, I've known police officers throughout my life, some even through familial ties. Should I sever these ties because of police accountability issues? Should I view every white person as a racist? This approach makes no sense to me.

As public servants, we should serve everyone, regardless of race, gender, sexual orientation, or walk of life. The mission that should unite all activists and advocates is justice. Yet, the journey toward justice isn't always harmonious. There are activists I've disagreed with, and there have been struggles to unite on common ground.

Fayetteville PACT has marched across different parts of the United States, advocating for various causes, such as the rights of the people of Palestine or against police misconduct in Durham. These experiences have highlighted the importance of unity and understanding that we are all one race, one people, fighting one fight.

Being an activist is not about seeking recognition or funds; it's about serving the community and providing hope. Despite the long road ahead, we know that there's a light at the end of the tunnel. We believe that justice will one day be served.

In my personal war room, I pray for guidance and the strength to be the voice of those unheard. Despite the achievements since the civil rights movement of 1965, we still have a long way to go. The journey towards true democracy and humanity must continue, and it starts with uniting as one and holding everyone accountable, especially those who are paid by the citizens.

I've experienced criticism firsthand during my time in the United States Army. In foreign lands, we were seen as occupiers and invaders, while back home, we were hailed as heroes. This duality is reflective of the struggle we face in our own backyards. The fight for democracy continues, both overseas and within our cities and counties. As a veteran, I often wonder, how many wars must we fight before we can truly say we have full democracy in the United States?

Justice is what we seek, a universal right that everyone should have access to. However, as an activist, I've come to accept that not every battle ends in victory. A loss for one family feels like a loss for all, and the pain is palpable, whether it's a case of abuse or police misconduct.

In seeking justice, different outcomes can arise. A family might receive monetary compensation, while another might see the arrest of a police officer. Yet, if there's no accountability, it feels like a loss in both cases. Regardless, we strive to support these families, offering services even after a verdict. Our fight for justice continues, even when we aren't marching or holding press conferences.

Sometimes, the quest for justice can be hampered by misinformation. Some people might withhold details out of embarrassment or fear. As activists, we ensure they feel comfortable and trust us to maintain confidentiality unless they wish otherwise. My work as an activist has, at times, caused fear and anxiety among my family, especially during protests or confrontations with the District Attorney's office. My family supports my work but worries about my safety. There have been instances of intimidation directed towards me and my loved ones, causing distress and impacting my focus on cases.

This tension has also had personal effects, particularly when I was dealing with my own medical issues. Despite undergoing therapy and managing physical illnesses, I remained steadfast in my pursuit of justice, often sidelining my own needs.

The common adage of self-care and self-love seems challenging in the face of injustice. How can I prioritize myself when families are suffering and justice is denied? How can we not fight against the harm inflicted on people's lives and families? Is it humane to believe that killing another person is acceptable?

In my opinion, many public servants have lost their way, succumbing to greed, recognition, and status. They fear humiliation or backlash for speaking out or taking action. Some attorneys even shy away from police misconduct cases, fearing damage to their reputation or business. This raises questions about whether these attorneys and officials are truly serving the public interest.

While there are civil rights attorneys who claim to be there to help families, much needs to be done to hold public servants accountable. In the underbelly of the justice system, lawyers have been seen to abandon families and cases when justice seems out of reach or when lucrative payouts wane. Even Judges, the supposed paragons of justice, have shockingly engaged in unethical conduct, threatening and belittling those wrongfully ensnared in the system.

I have been a firsthand witness to a judge wielding his gavel like a sword, threatening a 25-year sentence to an innocent client if they dared not accept a plea deal. This raises a question that casts a long shadow: are we fighting for justice within an inherently unjust system? Do judges shield the police? Are they truly servants of the public, or do they abuse their power, profiting from the pain of those who've been wronged?

Sadly, this isn't an isolated incident but a repeating pattern casting a grim shadow over our justice system. Are judges indispensable, or have they strayed too far from their noble purpose of dispensing justice? The Bible wisely cautions, *"Judge not, or you will be judged."* How, then, can we hold judges accountable and ensure they uphold justice impartially? It's disconcerting to know that some judges and attorneys might strike deals before a trial, disregarding the facts and the defense's perspective. The district attorney's role can be a game-changer, swaying charges, sentencing, and plea deals. Yet, discerning a fair judge or DA from a biased one can be akin to walking a tightrope.

One potential solution to this opaque problem is transparency. Providing public access to personnel records and files of public servants could expose any potential biases or misconduct. It could also offer a glimpse into the track record of those with the power to sway lives before they even step foot in a courtroom.

As veterans, we've been trained to never leave anyone behind, a value that extends beyond the battlefield. It's a principle we carry with us, helping those who lack the strength to continue on their own. I've seen this commitment in action, working with veterans during their transition out of service and with individuals who demonstrate the same dedication to advocacy work.

I'll focus on a recent loss in our ranks, former council member Ted Mohn, who passed away at the age of 59. Ted and I had many conversations that may have seemed cryptic to outsiders. We had a military understanding, an acknowledgment of the chain of command, but also a respect for the insights of the enlisted. Ted often reminded me that our mission could only succeed if we had allies on our side.

In the days following Ted's death, I wept. Ted was a good man who believed in doing what was right for the greater good of the people. He always stressed the importance of considering all factors before making decisions to avoid igniting division or separation.

Another veteran holds a special place in my heart, namely Assistant Chief Nolette.[21] His commitment to the law and the community was unwavering. He believed in maintaining open lines of communication and ensuring complete transparency between the Fayetteville PACT and him. I believe this connection stems from our shared military background. I trusted that Chief Nolette would foster relationships with organizations outside the

---

[21] National Institute of Justice. (n.d.). James Nolette. https://nij.ojp.gov/bio/james-nolette.

Police Department, which is why I passionately wanted him to be the next Chief of Police.

Yet, it's unfortunate to see the general perception of the police as inherently evil, particularly by groups who may not have had a military or law enforcement background. In any profession, there are individuals who do not uphold the standards and expectations of their role. As soldiers, we have seen this in the military with both troublesome soldiers and ineffective superiors, just as it can be observed within the police force. Leadership, in my view, starts at the top and trickles down. The public perception of police forces, sheriff's offices, fire departments, and other public entities is heavily influenced by the quality of leadership. Drawing from my personal encounters, I believe it's crucial to listen to diverse perspectives on police and authority figures. These insights, shared by my friends Ted Mohn, Kirk DeViere, Karla Icaza, and others, shaped my understanding of this complex issue.

Karla, one of my most trusted friends and a fierce advocate for the Latino community has taught me a great deal about how this community perceives authority figures, especially the police. She highlighted the disparities in the services offered to them, which are often less than favorable. Our mutual experiences serving together at Fort Bragg in 2006 built a strong bond of trust between us.

Karla also demonstrated the importance of collaboration between governmental and non-governmental entities in building a unified community. Our shared experiences with former Councilman Christopher Davis and other veterans helped us understand the power of collective action and its impact on the community.[22]

Despite the personal injustices they or their families may have suffered, activists must remain steadfast in their fight. They draw strength from various sources, and the battle for justice, especially regarding the police, continues for years, maybe even decades.

As civilians, it can be very frustrating to witness the injustice from those in power, from those who we brought into power. To be oppressed by those who were supposed to protect us. As justice warriors, the emotional toll can be daunting.

While much progress has been made, we have only barely scratched the surface. It's disheartening to see the prevalence of supremacy in some organizations, including black supremacy.[23] While white supremacy may be a reality in some nonprofit organizations and government departments, it's crucial to acknowledge that black supremacy, too, exists. This might come as a surprise, but the notion of black supremacy, as defined by Wikipedia, is a racially discriminatory ideology asserting the

---

[22] Thompson, M. (2019, October 31). Chris Davis is people-focused, purpose-driven. Fayobserver. https://www.fayobserver.com/story/opinion/columns/2019/10/31/thompson-chris-davis-is-people-focused-purpose-driven/2400013007/.

[23] Wikipedia contributors. (2021, December 18). Black supremacy. Wikipedia. https://en.wikipedia.org/wiki/Black_supremacy.

superiority of black people over other races. And this is not just a theoretical concept. I've personally experienced disputes with numerous organizations in North Carolina where this mindset prevails. Many activists in the region believe that the fight for their race takes precedence over any other. This belief fuels a sense of obligation to fight specifically for their race rather than for universal equality. Unfortunately, the fear of jeopardizing funding often silences open discussions about this issue.

As a part of the Fayetteville PACT, we have worked alongside various groups, including the Nation of Islam[24], the Huey Newton Gun Club, the Black Panthers[25], and Black United, all of which promote unity among black communities. These organizations operate under the belief that for black people to rise, unity within black and brown communities must come first.

While there is undoubtedly a need for unity and empowerment within marginalized communities, it's my firm belief that justice should be colorblind. It should be served to all races and faces. When all races unite and fight for justice collectively, it will be served to everyone —not just black and brown people. Ultimately, the fight for equality shouldn't be

---

[24] Nation of Islam. (n.d.). Official Website. https://noi.org/.

[25] Britannica, T. Editors of Encyclopaedia. (2021, August 22). Huey P. Newton. Encyclopedia Britannica. https://www.britannica.com/biography/Huey-P-Newton.

restricted to a particular race but should encompass all of humanity. The question of whether all races should unite in the fight for justice or whether we should continue advocating within our individual activist groups is a complex one for most people. The rise of George Floyd's case in 2020 left me perplexed, as I saw more white people than black people marching for justice in his name. It was puzzling to see foundations donating more funds to black organizations while other causes were left in the shadows. It made me question the motivations of these foundations and whether they were truly committed to equality or if they were merely seeking positive publicity.

Most activists who do not receive salary-based grants often feel compelled to abandon their cause. This is dispiriting, as the people they are fighting for may not know if their activists will stand with them throughout the battle. Not receiving compensation can be demotivating, even for celebrities who advocate for justice. Notably, many black celebrities fall short of supporting the cause both vocally and financially. Consider Jay-Z, who founded a nonprofit for people wrongfully accused or arrested by the police.[26] However, aside from Meek Mill's case, there haven't been many instances where this organization has actively sought justice. It seems that celebrities only become

---

[26] ABC News. (2019, January 23). Meek Mill and Jay-Z launch criminal justice reform organization 'to speak for all the people who don't have a voice.' ABC News.

https://abcnews.go.com/Politics/meek-mill-jay-launch-criminal-justice-refo rm-organization/story?id=60552751.

involved in police accountability when a case goes viral and involves high-profile individuals like attorney Ben Crump.[27]

In terms of civil rights organizations, the NAACP is a prominent voice. However, I was shaken by an incident in my local chapter where LGBTQA individuals were turned away due to their sexual orientation. This was contradictory to my understanding of the NAACP's mission, which I believed encompassed racial equity and disparities affecting people of all genders, races, and religions.

Activism, in my opinion, shouldn't be selective. We shouldn't pick and choose who we want to help based on their race, gender, or sexuality. True activism goes beyond donating items during the holiday season or providing temporary relief. It's about providing comprehensive and lasting support, regardless of who the person is.

Often, people misuse religion as an excuse to avoid helping others or justifying their selective generosity. However, we should apply the principles of our faith more sincerely. While biblical stories and sacrifices of others can be inspiring, would we be inspired enough to work toward the cause in spite of people's race or ethnicity? For instance, would we offer food, drink, or shelter to a stranger in need? In my experience, many

---

[27] Ben Crump. (n.d.). Trial Lawyer for Justice. https://bencrump.com/.

individuals aspire to serve the public but selectively choose who and what to help.

The struggle becomes real when I reach out to other self-proclaimed activists who refuse to help because the individual in need is not black or does not identify as straight. These activists often only step forward when a case goes viral or incites public unrest. They are quick to show support publicly, but their assistance often disappears once the spotlight fades.

True activism is not just about standing up for someone when the cameras are rolling. It's about being there even when the fire dies down, providing ongoing support and resources to those in need, regardless of their race, gender, or sexual orientation.

I firmly believe that no individual or group should incite or participate in riots. It's far more beneficial to engage in dialogue with those you disagree with, practicing self-control and respect. This approach not only fosters better understanding and resolution but also demonstrates a willingness to listen and collaborate rather than promoting conflict and division. In my experience, the reason many people, particularly government employees, do not engage in full-scale activism or advocacy is due to the constraints of their roles. Working for the government is different from working for a private company; government employees have additional obligations. They must adhere to specific protocols and uphold the oath they've taken, promising not to oppose the president or any branch of government.

This can present a dilemma for those who wish to engage in activism. It often comes down to choosing between the cause you believe in and the potential consequences of standing up for it. This was a conversation I had with Ted, who was a City Council member, a government employee, and a military veteran. Despite our disagreements with the president and his administration, as government employees, we had to accept that the president was our commander and could not publicly defy his orders.

As a federal government union member, I found it fascinating that there are specific rules outlining what you can and cannot advocate against. It puts you at a crossroads, forcing you to choose between your morals and your livelihood. Not every fight is our battle, and not every issue of police accountability is our fight.

Unfortunately, there seems to be an inclination among some people to fan the flames of hate. I'm unsure why this is the case, but it's a phenomenon that has persisted for decades, even before my time. The word *'hate'* is powerful, yet some people harbor such intense hatred that they cannot see past the information laid out before them. Some people allow their personal feelings of vengeance and hatred to cloud their judgment, leading them to involve themselves in situations without fully considering the consequences. As part of the Fayetteville PACT, I strive to avoid this. I cannot let my personal feelings or desire for revenge influence my involvement in any case or incident we review.

It's a struggle, as sometimes, as activists, we might inadvertently do more harm than good by focusing on our personal fight for justice rather than considering the broader picture. Yet, it's important to remember that justice should always be the end goal, and as long as we strive towards it, justice will prevail.

The fight for justice can strain relationships and friendships. It's an unfortunate reality that not everyone may understand or support your cause. However, standing up for what you believe in often demands tough sacrifices.

Surrounding yourself with like-minded individuals can provide much-needed support and shared values.

In the trenches of activism, the commitment to never abandon a comrade in need is a virtue held high. Yet, it's equally essential to prioritize self-care and seek support when necessary. Remember, you're not alone in this fight. The support of fellow activists, advocacy organizations, and mental health professionals can guide you through this challenging journey.

Ultimately, the decision to continue or step back from activism is deeply personal, hinging on your well-being, your impact so far, and your life goals. Remember, it's vital to prioritize your health and happiness. If your children express an interest in joining the fight for justice, it could be an enriching learning experience. Trust your intuition and choose the path that feels right for you. It's crucial to remember that change is often slow, and the path to justice is strewn with setbacks. It's through unity with fellow advocates and organizations that we can spotlight systemic issues and push for enduring reforms.

We must keep fighting for justice for everybody, no matter how much blood, sweat, or tears it takes. It's natural to question one's resilience and the odds of achieving justice. Activists might reach a point of questioning their potency. If there are no other people fighting with me, should I continue to fight? Do I end the fight if the family tells me they don't want to? Even though it's unlikely that these questions will ever have an answer, I ask myself them every day when I go to the DOJ and write a letter or show up to a county or city council meeting to protest.

As I engage with officials at the General Assembly to discuss proposed legislation, I can't help but wonder if I'm fighting for someone else or just myself. Will I become more passionate about each case by changing the tone of my voice? Should I lash out at people who ignore my letters or emails asking for help? With AI, how will this appear in the future?

Will families simply accept the information provided by internal affairs? Will I continue to fight for justice for people until my death? Will my family still be able to comprehend the sacrifices I have to make for strangers? Perhaps one day, I'll discover how my path is meant to conclude, or perhaps it will begin when I set out to mentor another activist.

In order to continue living our daily lives and to maintain our routines in the event that our activism comes to an end, activists must make many sacrifices. Will anyone assist us as we look across to see what remains after we leave? Will someone be available to assist those if I am not present?

It is a daily struggle I face, and I will keep using all of my strength and determination to help those in need as long as I see them. While my stance was questioned many times, I would like to clarify that the reason for this is not fame or wealth of any kind but rather my personal covenant with God and Jesus. I would also like to stress that you should never question your willingness to help someone else when you are in a combat situation where your life is in danger. I often wonder what the future holds for me as an activist and where I should be. But for now, I'll have to wait and see. The only thing that is certain is that I will continue to fight for what I believe in and for the betterment of our society.

Chapter 4: Today And Tomorrow

I often find myself at a crossroads, contemplating the path I've walked and the journey that lies ahead. Here, in the present moment, I am compelled to reevaluate my life's purpose and my role in the activist and human rights movements. As technology evolves and a new generation emerges, I am faced with a profound question:

Do I step aside and allow them to carry the torch, advocating for those I have fought for all these years? Or do I take on the responsibility of mentoring and coaching them, guiding their steps as they navigate the treacherous terrain of social change? In my journey as a rights activist, I have encountered countless individuals who have served as my mentors and coaches. Some started as adversaries, but through the transformative power of connection, we became allies. Nelson Mandela's words resonate deeply within me: "You can make your enemies your friends so the war can end." While I don't view this movement as a war, as an activist, I see myself as a soldier on a chessboard, engaged in a battle to tackle the goals and missions I have set out to achieve, enforce, implement, and ratify.

Even after leaving the military, my mind continues to perceive the world through a different lens. I approach every situation and challenge as though I am on a battlefield. To conquer what lies ahead, I must utilize every tool at my disposal, leveraging the battlefield itself to secure victory. It brings to mind the memory of a brother I met years ago, Brother Bernard Brooks. Our paths crossed while I was distributing flyers for a Fayetteville PACT at a local recreation center. In the black community, there is an undeniable sense of daring, a spirit that cannot be ignored.

As I reflect upon my past and peer into the future, I am filled with a mix of emotions. There is a sense of awe at the progress made, the battles fought, and the lives touched. But there is also a twinge of vulnerability, a realization that the time may come when I must pass the torch to the next generation. Yet, amidst these swirling emotions, one truth remains steadfast: the fight for justice and equality is far from over. It is a fight that demands our unwavering commitment and our unyielding passion. And so, I will continue to march forward, my footsteps guided by the lessons learned, the wisdom gained, and the fire that burns within me.

In this battlefield of activism, where victories are measured in hearts touched, and lives changed, I find solace and purpose. It is a calling that transcends time and circumstance, a mission that beckons me forward. As I navigate this ever-evolving landscape, I am reminded of the power we possess when we come together, when we transform enemies into allies, and when we dare to challenge the status quo.

The journey is far from over. With every step, every word, and every action, I strive to leave an indelible mark on the world, to create a future where justice reigns supreme, and equality knows no bounds. The battlefield awaits, and I am ready to fight.

Recently, I had the incredible opportunity to participate in a thought-provoking panel discussion alongside Nuri Muhammad, where we delved into ways to improve and build a stronger black community. Being the only panelist who belonged to another organization, I could sense a certain level of intimidation from some of the participants, most notably Brother Bernard Brooks from the Nation of Islam.

Having previously immersed myself in the study and daily attendance of the mosque in Philadelphia during the 1990s, Brother Brooks and I engaged in conversations that I believe will greatly contribute to my upcoming book series. These discussions not only provided invaluable insight but also shed light on the myriad ways we can organize, mobilize, and establish stability.

To foster a collective effort within the black community, it is imperative that we familiarize ourselves with all the organizations operating in our vicinity and understand their respective missions and objectives. One organization that I deeply respect is the Nation of Islam, as they exhibit exceptional discipline, prioritizing the safeguarding and education of their own community. They remain dedicated to teaching and refuse to leave the black community behind, even as they contemplate the infrastructure and dynamics of a separate black community distinct from white communities.

Whenever I seek a fresh perspective or contemplate how Fayetteville can contribute to the betterment of not only the black community but also the brown community, I make a point of engaging in conversations with Brother Mohammed. Additionally, Minister Ammon Muhammad, who presides over the mosque in Durham, has imparted invaluable teachings on discipline, order, and emotional control as an individual and as a leader. During one of our discussions, I highlighted the stark reality that black and brown people find themselves at a significant economic disadvantage, with a staggering 75-year gap in terms of development and generational wealth when compared to other races. According to my calculations, it would take us more than 125 years to catch up, even with the contribution of our esteemed celebrities, actors, and billionaires.

This disparity exists primarily because those in the black and brown communities who possess significant economic resources are often unwilling to invest in and collaborate with others or join forces to acquire land and build community hubs within their own neighborhoods.

In the wake of George Floyd's tragic death, we have witnessed a surge in diversity, with numerous organizations and corporations finally acknowledging the black community. We now see black individuals featured prominently in Walmart commercials, Dove advertisements, and even a movie like The Little Mermaid with a black lead actor.28 However, I am left wondering whether this newfound representation truly satisfies the black and brown community in terms of diversity, equity, and inclusion or whether it is merely a superficial attempt by these corporations, foundations, and organizations to pacify us with meager offerings.

Why did it require such a horrific event as George Floyd's death for us to finally feel like we belong? These are the questions I explore further in my upcoming series as I delve into the complexities of racism, colorism, and, yes, even capitalism. It is crucial to consider economics and race when examining capitalism, as eloquently stated by the renowned activist and scholar Dr. Angela Davis. Over the course of generations, capitalism has become innately intertwined with racism, hindering our progress in economic matters despite the significant accomplishments we have made thus far.29

As I sit here, pondering the plight of black and brown communities, my heart aches with both hope and despair. It is a bittersweet mix of emotions that consumes me, for I have seen

---

[28] Vox. (n.d.). The Little Mermaid remake: The racist backlash over increased diversity, explained. Retrieved from https://www.vox.com/culture/23357114/the-little-mermaid-racist-backlash-lotr-rings-of-power-diversity-controversy

[29] Truthout. (n.d.). How Capitalism and Racism Support Each Other. Retrieved from https://truthout.org/articles/how-capitalism-and-racism-support-each-other/

the struggles and the dreams of my people, and I have questioned the path that lies before us.

We often use the term "woke" to describe social awareness, but does it truly encompass the struggles faced by the black community? Does it extend to the brown community and the immigrant community? These are essential questions that demand thoughtful consideration. Genuine progress in these areas necessitates a comprehensive exploration of the complex intersectionality between race, economics, and societal structures.

The journey to uplift and empower the black and brown communities requires a collective effort, a thorough understanding of our shared principles, and a willingness to challenge existing systems. Only through unity, education, and a genuine commitment to economic advancement can we hope to bridge the gap and secure a brighter future for all.

This is my story, my battle, and my identity. I will continue shedding light on the intricacies of our collective experience and envisioning a future where true equality and justice prevail. It is through understanding, empathy, and a commitment to dismantling oppressive systems that we can forge a path toward genuine liberation.

In this world where not all are awakened, where unity and solidarity elude us, we yearn for something greater. We aspire to build empires that extend far beyond the boundaries of our own communities to establish a foundation of generational wealth. We strive for LLCs, nonprofits, and tax write-offs, believing they will pave the way to financial security. But is it enough? Can we truly guarantee the survival of our communities in the face of an ever-evolving landscape dominated by artificial intelligence?

It is a harsh reality that degrees, education, and even residing in affluent neighborhoods do not necessarily safeguard our future. This truth may be disheartening, but I refuse to surrender to despair. I choose to confront it head-on, armed with statistical evidence and my own observations.

To achieve genuine justice, we must delve deeper. We must explore economic strategies, revitalize our communities, and combat the relentless force of gerrymandering.[30] This insidious practice undermines our arguments for redistricting and clashes with the very foundations of our democracy. Racism and housing discrimination further compound these challenges, leaving us questioning our place in America.

Amidst all this, there are questions that eat me every day. Should we seek better opportunities for generational wealth in other nations? Should we invest our dreams in lands that promise brighter futures for our children and grandchildren? These questions have no easy answers, for the future remains a mystery unfolding before our eyes.

But I refuse to be swayed by the winds of confusion. I choose to fight. To fight for economic equality, for equal opportunity,

---

[30] WUNC. (2023, October 24). New district maps show signs of GOP partisan gerrymandering. Retrieved from https://www.wunc.org/politics/2023-10-24/new-district-maps-show-signs-of-gop-partisan-gerrymandering

and for the betterment of black and brown communities. We may not know where we will thrive the most, but together, through perseverance and unity, we will carve a path toward a brighter tomorrow.

Our journey may be uncertain and fraught with challenges and obstacles, but we will navigate it with unwavering determination. We will adapt to the changing tides, embracing the unknown with open arms, for we are resilient people bound by a shared history and a collective dream.

As we approach the year 2025, many people are still unprepared for the digital age that we're entering. With the introduction of the digital dollar, we will see a shift in economics and possibly even a recession. Despite the challenges we face, it's surprising to see how many people continue to live their lives as if COVID, recession, inflation, and racism don't exist. Some might call them the "unwoke." But there are others who are actively working to make our world a better place.

I had the privilege of working with individuals whose stories were hidden from the world. Conversations were held in quiet corners, and research delved into the depths of society's challenges. Together, we explored the restoration of reentry society, shining a light on the struggles faced by those seeking a fresh start. Domestic violence became a topic of intense discussion as we sought to understand its complexities and find ways to break the cycle.

One individual, Councilwoman Kathy Jensen for District 1, proved to be an unexpected ally in this pursuit of justice. We've had many conversations about important issues that affect women, such as domestic violence and breast cancer. In fact, I vividly remember a conversation I had with Kathy about equal pay for women. We both agreed that equal pay across the board doesn't exist for women, but the gap is even wider for black women. It was shocking to discover that Hispanic women are paid more than black women because they're considered a minority, which led us to ask the question: who is really the minority now?

Have you ever wondered why we still argue about equal rights and pay for women? It has been going on for decades, yet we still haven't reached a definitive solution. But what if we shifted the conversation to argue for equal pay for all, regardless of gender or race? That conversation still has me caught up to this day. Councilwoman Kathy Jensen and I have bumped heads in the past, but this particular conversation was different. We talked for 30 minutes, and I got a new perspective on the issue.

We delved into the rate of pay for women, not just in the $35,000 to $50,000 range but also in the $20,000 to $30,000 range. We discussed how this fight for equal pay is not just a federal and state issue but also a policy issue. We looked at how we're approaching equal rights for women, particularly in regard to the ERA. The conversation left me thinking, what if we focused on equal pay for all? It's time we move past arguing about which group is considered a minority and work toward a solution that benefits everyone. We need to realize that the fight for equal pay is not (and should not be) limited to a single group but is a battle for all.

This reminds me of another person, County Commissioner Jim Keefe. The weight of our conversation settled upon me like a burden that I couldn't shake off. We delved deep into the topic of reentry in Cumberland County, discussing the struggles faced by those leaving the confines of the county detention center and returning home.

We acknowledged the pressing need for transitional housing, a safe haven to guide individuals through the arduous process of reintegration. We recognized that a mere release from jail was not enough; these individuals deserved a chance to rebuild their lives. That's when it hit us — the importance of treatment centers, rehabilitation facilities, and substance abuse programs. These programs were crucial to helping people get back on their feet after leaving the Cumberland County detention center.

But our intentions were not without obstacles. The reentry society, a group of individuals seeking redemption, faced a distinct challenge. Bound by their past actions, they found themselves excluded from shelters and other facilities, as they were classified as ex-sexual offenders. It begged the question: why should they be separated? If second chances truly exist, then why couldn't we bridge the gap between those who had stumbled and those who hadn't?

Commissioner Keefe and I shared a vision — a vision that surpassed judgment and embraced compassion. We were getting funding from the federal and state governments for reentry programs. We recognized the need to provide specialized services for this specific group, tailoring our efforts to their unique circumstances. It wasn't about segregating the homeless community; it was about empowering those who had fallen to rise again. As a human rights activist, I firmly believe that everyone, without exception, deserves a second chance. After all, who were we to pass judgment upon others? We were all flawed, all susceptible to mistakes. It was time to redefine the concept of a true servant, harkening back to the teachings of Jesus himself.

But our discussions didn't end there; they extended to the realm of education. I pondered the future of our youth, burdened by the weight of financial obligations and the scarcity of scholarships. Would they still have the opportunity to pursue their dreams? Or would they succumb to the hardships faced by previous generations, where education took a backseat to survival?

Education had always been a contentious issue in the United States, and as a human activist, it was a question that lingered in my mind. The term "school-to-prison pipeline" echoed, but I recoiled at the derogatory nature of such a phrase, particularly when it disproportionately affected black and brown children. It was a term that sought to divide, to label some as "at risk" and deny them their right to education.

But the roots of this injustice ran deep, intertwined with the very fabric of our history. I couldn't help but recall the stories of Emmett Till and the young black boy accused of a crime he didn't commit, becoming the youngest black boy executed in America. The school-to-prison pipeline had roots that reached far back, back to a time when runaway slaves and petty crimes on black youth shaped the course of their lives. As I closed my conversation with Commissioner Keefe, I was thrilled that I was able to even make a pinch of change. We had spoken of second chances of compassion and of breaking the chains that held our society back. It was a battle I was willing to fight, armed with the power of words, empathy, and an unyielding belief in the inherent worth of every individual. The journey was far from over, but I was determined to make a difference — one life at a time.

    I often find myself contemplating the future, wondering how it will shape the landscape of education. With the emergence of AI police, a new era seemed to be dawning—one where artificial intelligence would oversee our schools. But what implications would this hold? Would AI police officers become a common sight in our classrooms? And if so, which levels and grades would they oversee?

    As I pondered these questions, my thoughts inevitably turned to the 14th Amendment and the ongoing battle against the school-to-prison pipeline. Could a reevaluation of this constitutional provision pave the way for a more just system? Could it provide the structure and support needed to ensure that black youth could pursue their education without the looming threat of criminalization and profiling? It was no secret that black and brown youth often faced harsher treatment within public schools, leading to higher arrest rates, racial profiling, and increased disciplinary actions. The presence of School Resource Officers (SROs) seemed to exacerbate these issues. But would changing the 14th amendment and implementing more programs in communities like Fayetteville be enough to eliminate the need for SROs in schools?

The issue of gun violence loomed large in this discussion. Across the United States, schools have been marred by tragic incidents, often due to a lack of accountability in the parent-child relationship or the shortcomings of the social service system. It was a harsh reality, highlighting the flaws in our societal structures meant to protect and nurture our youth. Failed programs meant to support SROs and counselors in schools only added to the complexity of the situation.

In some states, the idea of arming teachers had even been considered as a response to the threat of active shooters on campuses. But as I weighed the potential risks and liabilities, it became clear that the value placed on funding far outweighed the lives of students—a disheartening reflection of our capitalist society.

Should we allow ourselves to continue down this path, where our children and teachers become collateral damage in the fight against gun violence? Could AI police be the solution? Would they be able to detect potential threats, counsel students, and ensure the safety of our educational institutions? And if schools were no longer used for their intended purpose, who would be held accountable?

These questions weighed heavily on my mind, especially as the COVID-19 pandemic reshaped the landscape of education. Many teachers chose to leave the profession, seeking safer alternatives, as the risk of active shooters became yet another threat to their well-being. The rise of online schooling further complicated matters, with parents opting for remote learning over the traditional classroom setting, even at the college level.

It seemed that for some communities, schools no longer provided a comprehensive solution for their children's growth and development in society. Technology has become a dominant force, shaping the way our children think and interact. Platforms like texting, TikTok, Snapchat, Facebook, and Instagram held more allure than the pages of a book. Education, once a gateway to understanding and growth, now faced competition from the digital realm.

As I contemplated these changes, I couldn't help but wonder—what had become of the true essence of learning? Was it slowly being overshadowed by the distractions of modern technology? And if so, how could we reclaim its importance in our society?

The future held both promise and uncertainty with the advent of AI police and the ever-evolving role of technology. It was a landscape that demanded careful navigation and critical examination. As a human rights activist, I knew that the answers lay not in surrendering to fear or abandoning education but in finding a balance—a balance that preserves the safety of our children while upholding their right to learn and grow.

However, education is not just about the specific curriculum or major one pursues. It is a process of understanding, a means of acquiring knowledge that could be applied in various aspects of life. My own family, despite holding degrees, had found themselves utilizing the skills gained from those degrees in different career paths. In fact, statistics showed that nearly 48% of college graduates did not end up using their degrees in their chosen careers. Instead, they pursued higher education to enhance their chances of promotion within their existing fields.

But as I delved deeper into the complexities of our education system, a troubling thought emerged—were we inadvertently fueling the flames of racism within this structure? Capitalism seemed to play a significant role, intertwining with the very fabric of our educational institutions. I couldn't help but recall a conversation with my mother, who had taught me the game of chess after my return from Iraq in 2008. At the time, I resisted, feeling as though my life was already trapped on a chessboard. But my mother insisted, stating that understanding the value and strategic use of each piece on the board was akin to understanding the tactics employed by politicians. She emphasized that politics, like a game of chess, held significant sway over our lives. If we failed to recognize ourselves as players on this chessboard, we would become mere pawns in the game, subject to the whims and decisions made by those in power.

It was a sobering realization. Our livelihoods, our equality, and our way of life were all at stake. Democracy, I understood, rested in the hands of the people, but only if the people recognized the fight they were in. Over the years, as I immersed myself in this work, I encountered individuals who had little understanding of the criminal justice system, the education system, or the reentry system. It often took personal experiences or stories from their own families or acquaintances to shed light on the inequalities and racial disparities that permeated these systems.

I was reminded of the exorbitants associated with expungement—a process that could range from $10,000 to $20,000 just to file a petition. This, once again, highlighted the influence of capitalism within the criminal justice system. Individuals leaving jail or detention centers were burdened with restitution, court fees, and probation fees. If they lacked the financial means to fulfill these obligations, they risked returning to jail. It was a vicious cycle, contributing to the school-to-prison pipeline, where youth who had experienced detention centers found themselves in trouble again, caught in the grip of habitual criminal activities.

Sadly, this was a direct result of capitalism. The prison system, an organization funded by private investors and government resources, thrived on the wealth generated by the youth, especially black and brown individuals and those entangled within the prison system. Restitution payments flowed back into the system, enriching not only the jails but also the county, city, federal government, and state. It became clear that the United States of America profited from the incarceration of its own citizens.

The prison system itself was a business model, with private prisons contracted by the government to operate facilities. Critics argued that such privatization led to unjust conditions and corruption, questioning how a private company could legally imprison individuals when it seemed to be the government's responsibility.

As I reflected on these troubling realities, I couldn't help but feel a sense of urgency. The chessboard of capitalism is rigged against us, and it is time to challenge the status quo. Education, the true essence of learning and understanding, needs to be reclaimed from the clutches of distractions and technological allure. We are in a battle for our rights, our equality, and our future.

In the ever-changing landscape of our criminal justice system, the role of prisons has undergone a significant transformation. While public prisons remain under government ownership and administration, they rely on private contractors for certain services like food, cleaning, and maintenance. Private prisons, on the other hand, are profit-driven entities aiming to generate revenue from their operations.

To secure their funds, private prisons enter into contracts with both the government and the corporation that oversees them. These contracts outline the payment terms and the basis for compensation. For example, if it costs the government $100 per day to incarcerate a person and the private prison offers to do it for $150 per day, the government may agree to the terms if it results in cost savings compared to running a public prison.

The economics behind private prisons can be appealing on the surface, but the issue lies in the inherent conflict of interest. While cost savings may be achieved, the profit-driven nature of private prisons raises concerns about the quality of care and rehabilitation provided to incarcerated individuals. This is where the role of AI comes into play. As we enter the digital age, the question arises: will AI be used in both public and private prisons? Will the presence of AI police replace human officers? And how will this impact the treatment of prisoners? These are complex questions that warrant careful consideration.

The potential benefits of AI in prisons are vast. AI technology can enhance surveillance capabilities, utilizing facial recognition, shot spotters, and other crime prevention initiatives.[31] It can streamline investigative practices and improve efficiency within law enforcement agencies. The rapid expansion of surveillance capabilities has reshaped the way investigators produce reasonable suspicion, relying on accurate data traces from everyday life rather than solely on past criminal records.

But as we embrace these advancements, we must also consider the implications for human rights and the protection of prisoners. The United Nations Office on Drugs and Crime acknowledges that the digital age has witnessed an increase in technology-enabled crimes, as well as the development and deployment of technology for crime prevention and control. This poses a challenge in ensuring the balance between crime prevention and safeguarding human rights. While technology can undoubtedly aid in crime prevention, we must tread carefully to avoid infringing upon individual liberties. The use of AI in prisons raises questions about the potential for increased surveillance and the potential for AI systems to treat prisoners differently than human officers. It becomes crucial to establish clear guidelines and regulations to ensure that the implementation of AI in prisons aligns with principles of fairness and justice.

As society evolves, fueled by advancements in technology, it is essential to consider the future of our criminal justice system.

---

[31] Prison Policy Initiative. (2021, June 8). New data: State prisons are increasingly deadly places. Retrieved from https://www.prisonpolicy.org/blog/2021/06/08/prison_mortality/

Will prisons continue to exist as we navigate the digital age? Will crime rates change, influenced by increased surveillance and technological interventions? These are complex issues that require thoughtful deliberation and consideration of the potential consequences.

The path forward lies in striking a balance between technological advancements and the preservation of human rights. As we explore the possibilities presented by AI in prisons, we must ensure that the dignity and well-being of incarcerated individuals remain at the forefront of our discussions and decision-making processes.

Despite reasonable warning about the potential in-services and prejudicial character of data-driven policing technology and how they reduce long-standing society and qualities, its use remains controversial. It has reaped both praise and criticism. While these technologies have the potential to reduce bias and improve policing practices, recent studies have highlighted the influence of past biases in data collection methods. Bittner's 1967 article on policing Skid Row sheds light on the relationship between policing work, law enforcement technologies, and the social structures that shape everyday life.

Bittner emphasizes that police officers acquire knowledge about the social structures of their beats as a response to the demands of their work. However, he also acknowledges that officers cannot possess factual knowledge about every person, place, or event. Instead, they develop area knowledge, which serves as a provisional scheme of interpretation, allowing them to connect the known with the unknown.

As we consider the future of policing in the context of artificial intelligence (AI), important questions arise. Can the police effectively train AI, or will AI train the police? In Chapter 2, we explored these questions, acknowledging that the integration of AI into policing raises complex issues regarding the interaction between AI and human officers within the criminal justice system. While ongoing research seeks to shed light on these matters, there is still much to learn about how AI will shape the future of policing and its relationship with human officers.

The tragic death of George Floyd and the subsequent movement for justice and police reform have led to the introduction of various policies and bills. However, as of 2023, only certain bills have been signed into law, while others, such as the George Floyd Justice in Policing Act, remain pending. The movement brought attention to police misconduct, brutality, and racial disparities, as well as systemic issues like white supremacy.[32]

Funding has been allocated to organizations, corporations, and police departments for diversity, equity, and inclusion training. However, the potential rise of AI in policing raises questions about the purpose and effectiveness of such training. Will AI also receive training regarding diversity, equity, and

---

[32] NBC News. (n.d.). Here's what the George Floyd Justice in Policing Act would do. Retrieved from https://www.nbcnews.com/politics/congress/here-s-what-george-floyd-justice-policing-act-would-do-n1264825

inclusion? These are important considerations as we navigate the evolving landscape of policing. One significant aspect of police reform discussions is the concept of qualified immunity. While some states have passed laws addressing qualified immunity, these laws often have limitations. Qualified immunity shields government officials from lawsuits alleging a violation of a person's rights, allowing lawsuits only when officials violate clearly established statutory or constitutional rights.

The need to reevaluate qualified immunity arises from cases where justice has been denied, even when excessive force was used. Examples include cases where individuals were shot multiple times by officers, mistaken identity led to fatal shootings, or individuals were left permanently injured. In these cases, courts ruled in favor of the police, citing qualified immunity as a defense against liability.

Congresswoman Ayanna Pressley has advocated for the elimination of qualified immunity, highlighting the need for justice and accountability. The current trend of the court's ruling in favor of police officers in excessive force cases underscores the urgency to reassess the application of qualified immunity.

As discussions and debates continue, it is clear that challenging the status quo is necessary to address the systemic issues within our policing and criminal justice systems. Reevaluating the role of technology, advocating for accountability, and promoting equity and justice are crucial steps toward creating a fair and unbiased system that serves and protects all members of society. Congresswoman Ayanna Pressley has introduced the Ending Qualified Immunity Act, which seeks to amend Section 1983 to explicitly state that qualified immunity does not protect police officers who violate civil rights.[33] The aim is to clarify Congress's original intent for Section 1983 and address the historical necessity of this protection.

However, it is important to note that qualified immunity extends beyond just police officers. It also applies to other officials, including judges and members of the Supreme Court. Qualified immunity shields these individuals from liability when they violate constitutional and civil rights. This raises questions about accountability and whether qualified immunity should be entirely eliminated.

One argument against ending qualified immunity is the potential impact it could have on other officials, such as attorneys, district attorneys, and judges. The concern is that eliminating qualified immunity may lead to increased personal liability and interfere with the confidentiality and functioning of the legal profession. It is important to consider the potential consequences and complexities associated with such a change. Furthermore, the elimination of qualified immunity could have significant implications for the criminal justice system. It would require individuals currently in prison to be released and

---

[33] House.gov. (2023, April 19). Pressley, Markey Announce Legislation to End Qualified Immunity. Retrieved from https://pressley.house.gov/2023/04/19/pressley-markey-announce-legislation-to-end-qualified-immunity/

potentially result in restitution for crimes in which individuals were coerced or forced to confess. Police officers may also face personal financial burdens if they have to pay for their own legal representation in cases where qualified immunity no longer applies. This could impact the officers' livelihoods and potentially reduce the number of police officers within their ranks.

It is crucial to ensure fairness and impartiality when considering changes to qualified immunity. While police officers may benefit from the protection of qualified immunity, it is also important to address issues of corruption and accountability within the entire justice system. The system must be designed in a way that is fair and unbiased for all individuals involved, including police officers, judges, and attorneys.

Ending qualified immunity is a complex endeavor that requires careful consideration of the potential consequences and the need for comprehensive reform. It is essential to evaluate the impact on all parties involved and strive for a system that upholds constitutional rights, civil rights, and equality under the law. As we reflect on the recent movements for police accountability, it is clear that there is still much work to be done. While measures like the "8 Can't Wait" campaign aim to address issues of excessive force, police brutality, and the use of chokeholds, true reform requires a comprehensive examination of police policies and practices.

The United States must continue to learn from past incidents and strive for a justice system that is fair, just, and accountable to all its citizens. This may involve reevaluating and rebuilding our legal framework to address the complexities and challenges that arise in the pursuit of justice and equality.

As the co-founder of my nonprofit organization, I have had the privilege of engaging with the citizens of Fayetteville, NC and witnessing their perspectives on the city, the county, and the North Carolina General Assembly. It is disheartening to see that it often takes tragic incidents like the deaths of George Floyd and Breonna Taylor for Congress and local officials to take a closer look at our police departments. However, these events have sparked important conversations about the future of policing, including the potential rise of AI police departments.

I believe that passing legislation is crucial to protect individuals' rights and hold police departments accountable for any misconduct or violations related to AI technology. We need bills that explicitly address these concerns and establish clear guidelines and mechanisms for oversight. Transparency measures and strict regulations should be in place to ensure that AI is used responsibly and in a manner that respects individuals' rights.

Throughout my journey, I have encouraged citizens to actively participate in their local government meetings and attend sessions of the North Carolina General Assembly. It is essential to understand the legislative process, policies, and procedures to effectively advocate for change and hold officials accountable. By familiarizing ourselves with previous ordinances, bills, and meeting archives, we can gain insights into voting patterns and the positions of individual officials.

As a nonprofit organization leader, I have undergone training from various organizations, each providing valuable perspectives and approaches. This training has equipped me with the tools and knowledge to advocate for our community effectively. We have prioritized ensuring that every citizen's voice is heard, and we have achieved measurable outcomes in areas like community policing.[34]

I have also witnessed organizations exercising their First Amendment rights by attending General Assembly sessions and speaking out against bills that they perceive as racist or sexist. It is essential for citizens to understand the political landscape, recognizing that North Carolina currently has a majority of Republicans in the General Assembly. Furthermore, the recent loss of forty Democratic seats in 2022 highlights the need for continued engagement and advocacy.

I firmly believe that individuals from all backgrounds should consider running for office. Public service is open to anyone who is passionate about serving their community and making a positive impact. Training programs can provide aspiring leaders with the necessary skills and knowledge to represent their constituents effectively.

As a United States Army soldier, I have learned the importance of leadership and the impact it has on the lives of

---

[34] ABC11. (n.d.). Fayetteville City Council moves forward with Community Police Advisory Board. Retrieved from https://abc11.com/community-police-advisory-board-fayetteville-review-city-council-citizens/10762770/

those under my command. Leading troops into war and ensuring their safe return to their families is an experience that will stay with me forever. This sense of duty and commitment extends to my work as a co-founder of Fayetteville PACT, where we have made the decision to rely on volunteers who understand that their efforts will not be compensated financially. Instead, Fayetteville PACT focuses on securing grants for the work we provide to other organizations, offering services to family members impacted by social injustices, and contributing funds to organizations that provide free services to citizens.

During my time with Fayetteville PACT, I had a conversation with retired Judge Weeks about the bail policies in Cumberland County Detention Center. We discovered that the detention center was not following the scheduled bail bond policy. This prompted discussions about the possibility of a lawsuit against Cumberland County for failing to adhere to the bail bond scheduling policy. We are committed to informing individuals held in the detention center about their rights, specifically their Eighth Amendment right to request a reduction in bail at any time. Unfortunately, many citizens are unaware of their rights and often rely on appointed attorneys without fully understanding the implications of the charges, sentencing, and plea deals.

One case that stands out is from 2022, where a man was accused of molesting his girlfriend's daughter and spent nine months in the detention center during the COVID-19 pandemic. Through the work of a private investigator, we discovered that the man's girlfriend was a correctional officer at the detention center and had fabricated the allegations out of anger and revenge. Despite having evidence to prove his innocence, the appointed attorney advised the client to accept a plea deal to avoid a potentially lengthy sentence. The client, traumatized and wanting to go home, made the difficult decision to accept the plea deal, resulting in time served, registration as a sex offender for 15 years, and ten years of probation.

This case raises important questions about the criminal justice system, the challenges of plea deals, and the impact on individuals' lives post-release. It is disheartening to see individuals compelled to accept plea deals due to the overwhelming trauma and shock of the charges without fully understanding the long-term consequences; reintegrating into society after incarceration presents numerous challenges, including homelessness, difficulty finding employment, and the burden of restitution. These factors often contribute to a cycle of recidivism, perpetuating the individual's involvement in the criminal justice system.

I have come to realize the significant cost of plea deals, both for the individuals involved and for the pursuit of justice. As an activist, I question the purpose of hiring a private investigator or advocating for innocence if a client ultimately decides to accept a plea deal. However, it is important to understand the complex circumstances individuals face and the difficult choices they make in hopes of reuniting with their families. The criminal justice system plays a pivotal role in shaping the lives of those who have been incarcerated, and the challenges of reintegration must be addressed to ensure a fair and just society.

Through my experiences, I have learned to caution against certain attorneys in North Carolina who may not prioritize the protection of civil rights or constitutional rights. It is essential to seek legal counsel who is committed to upholding these rights and advocating for justice.

The criminal justice system is supposed to serve justice, but the reality is much more complicated than that. Corruption runs deep, and it can be hard to know who to trust. Attorneys often advise their clients to plead guilty because they have connections with the District Attorney. Unfortunately, corruption among District Attorneys and judges can heavily influence the outcome of a case. District Attorneys are responsible for deciding the charges, sentencing, and whether a plea bargain is an option.

We must also address the issue of abuse of power by district attorneys and judges. Yes, you read that right. District attorneys and judges are not immune to corruption or conflicts of interest. We need to hold all public servants accountable and establish proper oversight to ensure that justice is truly served.

District attorneys have a lot of power in the criminal justice system, and they often work closely with attorneys and judges. This can create a conflict of interest that can have serious consequences for the accused.

The problem is that most people don't understand their rights and are at the mercy of the system. Attorneys may encourage clients to take a plea deal rather than fight for their rights, and many people don't even know that they have the right to a trial by a grand jury. This is where Fayetteville PACT comes in.

Fayetteville PACT is an organization that understands the power dynamics at play in the criminal justice system. They have received training that shows just how much power district attorneys and sheriffs have. For example, district attorneys can charge and even prosecute police officers. This means that they have a lot of control over what happens in the courtroom.

But it's not just district attorneys that have power. Sheriffs also play a crucial role in the criminal justice system. They are responsible for enforcing the law, and they can only be relieved of their duties if the district attorney decides to charge them. This creates a system where everyone is looking out for their own interests rather than for justice. Fayetteville PACT has even hired a private investigator to help them understand how the criminal justice system works. This investigator is an army veteran who has been doing investigations for over 30 years. He has worked with CID and has extensive experience in forensics. Together with the investigator, Fayetteville PACT has gone on several outings to gather evidence and learn more about how the system works.

The investigator, Michael Sheehan, is a valuable asset to the organization. He has the authority to testify in court, and he knows how to gather evidence that can be used to fight back against corrupt officials. This is important work, but it's not easy. The criminal justice system is complex, and it can be hard to know where to start.

They may have conflicts of interest when they have personal relationships with other attorneys, sheriffs, or deputies outside of the workplace. Why haven't we addressed this issue? Why haven't we investigated the relationships between district attorneys, local attorneys, or even judges?

We cannot be hypocritical by only focusing on policing police officers. We must hold all public servants accountable and establish oversight. What oversight exists for district attorneys? Who is present when a district attorney and a judge make decisions about what charges should be filed? With the rise of AI in the digital age, will we still have judges presiding over cases? Will constitutional law and civil rights continue to be upheld? How does AI in the digital age influence the implementation of laws and bills? If Fayetteville PACT were to stop policing the police, who would take on that responsibility in the city of Fayetteville? I have posed this question to several individuals who run their own nonprofits in Fayetteville, and most of them have expressed that they are not worried about the police but rather concerned about their own livelihoods. However, public safety, which is closely tied to how we are policed, affects the livelihoods we strive for. Every aspect of life is essential, and everyone has a role to play. How do we hold each other accountable without questioning our rights in court?

That's why it's so important for citizens to understand their rights and to fight for them. Constitutional law is not always practiced when you are under criminal charges, but that doesn't mean that you don't have rights. It's up to you to execute those rights and to demand justice.

As activists, we often find ourselves caught between a rock and a hard place. On one hand, we want to give hope to those who seek our assistance in dealing with trauma or the impact of social injustice. On the other hand, we have to confront the reality that not all cases require justice in the traditional sense.[35] Sometimes, financial compensation may be the best possible outcome for a victim. As Fayetteville PACT continues to grow and evolve, we have learned from experience that we cannot advocate for every case that comes our way. We need to review each case thoroughly and determine which ones are truly worth our time and effort.

Despite encountering fake news or news that does not provide a complete picture of internal investigations, we ensure that we have all the information before advocating for justice. The only reliable and comprehensive source of news in North Carolina that shows the full investigation is Gerald Jackson, an independent online news reporter called the NCBeat. He never alters the stories he receives and he never pressures families to come forward. Fayetteville PACT usually reaches out to him directly.

One important thing to keep in mind is that not all police officers are racist or have malicious intent toward people of color. Training plays a significant role in how police officer

---

[35] Civilytics. (2021). Myths & Realities of Local Budgets + The Cost of Policing. Retrieved from https://www.civilytics.com/posts/2021/myths-and-realities-of-local-budgets-and-the-cost-of-policing/

performs their duties, but we must also consider the work environment they are in. Hostile work environments greatly impact how a police officer interacts with individuals on the street. It's important to acknowledge this fact and not paint all police officers with the same brush.

While my personal history may not be widely known, I have had family members who served on the police force or as correctional officers. I have also been around military police during my time in the military at Fort Bragg, NC. I have friends who are currently serving as police officers in the civilian sector. Therefore, I have gained an understanding that the environment and cultural awareness play a significant role in how they interact with individuals.

In the age of AI and digitalization, we must also consider how these advancements will impact the implementation of laws and bills. Will constitutional law and civil rights continue to be upheld? What role will judges play in the future? These are all important questions that we need to start asking ourselves.

It's worth discussing the significance of life insurance and how it could potentially affect instances of excessive force and police brutality. If every citizen had life insurance policies, would police officers still use excessive force? After all, life insurance policies would have to pay out to the individuals' families in the event of their death. It's an interesting concept to consider and one that could potentially lead to a reduction in police brutality incidents.

I have known Laura Hardy since 2014 in Fayetteville, where she has evolved with her own LLC called the Laura Hardy Group.

Her work involves not only selling life insurance but also building assisted living centers. Life insurance is something that many people overlook when it comes to investments. People often invest in LLCs, nonprofits, and businesses but fail to prioritize life insurance.

I mention this in relation to qualified immunity. You may have thought I forgot about it, but I didn't. The reason I mentioned how Laura Hardy sells life insurance is that if everyone had life insurance for themselves and their family members, would police officers still use excessive force or engage in police brutality?

After all, life insurance policies would have to pay out to the individuals' families in the event of their death. I know this may seem far-fetched, but let's consider it. If every citizen had life insurance policies, would it potentially reduce instances of excessive force and eliminate qualified immunity for police officers? Why wouldn't people want life insurance for their family members?

Even in some countries, prison is not just punishment but also death. El Salvador has the highest prison rate globally and the highest murder rate, surpassing 50 per 100,000 inhabitants in 2022. Many countries with high homicide rates are located in Latin America. The United States has the second-largest number of prisoners worldwide, only surpassed by China. In 2023, approximately 1.68 million people were incarcerated in the U.S., while China had an estimated prison population of 1.69 million that year. Other nations had significantly fewer prisoners.

In the U.S., the majority of prisoners in federal correctional facilities were of African-American origin. As of 2020, there were 345,500 black, non-Hispanic prisoners compared to 327,300 white, non-Hispanic inmates. The states with the highest number of prisoners in 2021 were Texas, California, and Florida. Among sentenced prisoners in state facilities, over 160,000 were convicted of rape or sexual assault, making it the most common cause of imprisonment. Murder was the second most common offense, followed by aggravated or simple assault.

The Thirteenth Amendment to the U.S. Constitution abolished slavery throughout the country when ratified in 1865. However, in the documentary, Jelani Cobb argues that the amendment created a "loophole" allowing the massive criminalization of blackness, which has persisted from the era of Jim Crow to the prison industrial complex.

The Thirteenth Amendment's "exception clause" does not actively promote incarceration but ensures that the prohibition on racial slavery does not extend to criminal incarceration. The amendment aimed to end the holding of people as property and did not intend to erase the distinction between slavery and incarceration.[36] The overpopulation of prisons and the impact of

---

[36] Change.org. (n.d.). Petition · Establish Oversight Demystifying the 13th Amendment and Its Impact on Mass Incarceration - AAIHSBoards for Fayetteville (NC) Police!! · Change.org. Retrieved from https://www.change.org/p/mayor-mitch-colvin-establish-oversight-boards-for-fayetteville-nc-police

capitalism are interconnected. Despite the loss of many black and brown lives due to police violence, there has been limited progress in ratifying the Amendments and the Civil Rights Act.

A potential solution could involve allowing defendants to petition the court for constitutional rights and civil rights violations that occurred during their arrest before facing criminal charges. Additionally, implementing laws that allow all citizens to petition for a grand jury could be beneficial.

Taxpayers continue to bear the burden of funding equipment, staffing, and infrastructure for local detention centers or county jails. Instances like the killing of a protester in Atlanta, Georgia, at Cop City highlight the need for accountability and transparency in police training camps. Diversity, Equity, and Inclusion (DEI) training infrastructure and workforce development initiatives have been implemented, but their effectiveness in reducing police violence and eliminating hostile work environments in police departments remains uncertain. The end of affirmative action in higher education by the US Supreme Court in 2023 has sparked debates on the need for DEI enforcement instead. Affirmative action focuses on equal treatment without regard to race, color, religion, sex, or national origin, while DEI emphasizes individual/group differences, cultural distinctions, and physical characteristics associated with groups. Activist groups and organizations have protested the Supreme Court's decision, concerned about its impact on minorities and women applying for colleges.

Understanding the systems and corporations that govern us is crucial. The connection between capitalism, racism, and civil asset forfeiture laws is evident. Several states have scaled back their civil asset forfeiture laws since 2014.

However, the equitable sharing program allows state and local law enforcement to partner with the U.S. Justice and Treasury departments, transferring seized property to the federal government and receiving up to 80% of the proceeds from the sale, regardless of state law. This program has raised concerns about the violation of individual rights and the misuse of funds. For example, in North Carolina, a police officer conducting a traffic stop might seize $20,000 in cash from a vehicle, suspecting it to be related to drug activity. Even if the officer does not charge the driver with a crime, federal authorities may adopt the case and initiate forfeiture proceedings, returning 80% of the cash to the officer's agency. The Equitable Sharing program is detailed in the United States Department of Justice's "Guide to Equitable Sharing for State and Local Law Enforcement Agencies" (2009).

Since the COVID-19 pandemic, many people have struggled to make ends meet and live paycheck to paycheck. As a result, they are unable to afford life insurance policies for themselves and their families. Even though COVID-19 is still present in the United States and may continue to be for some time, how will it impact the future in terms of affordable housing, workforce development, and education?

Are we saying it's okay to continue being in debt as individuals while taxes and inflation are increasing, and people's jobs are at risk of being shut down or terminated because they can no longer afford rent?[37] Will the United States of America actually enter a full recession, becoming the poorest country? How can we know? Will history repeat itself, especially when AI takes over millions of jobs and lifestyles? I mention history because artificial intelligence remains a continuous controversy, with uncertainties about its future appearance in the next 50 or even 10 years. If artificial intelligence can detect intoxication and cannabis usage faster than a police officer conducting a breathalyzer test, as shown by a study conducted at Stanford University where 85% accuracy was achieved, what does this mean for the future of jobs for human beings when AI is fully implemented in all industrial and manufacturing companies?[38] Will humanity even exist in the future? When will we become extinct?[39]

---

[37] ABC11 Raleigh-Durham. (n.d.). Rental assistance programs continue to face backlogs. Rental assistance programs continue to face backlogs - ABC11 Raleigh-Durham

[38] The US Sun. (n.d.). New AI can detect if humans have smoked cannabis and 'alert medical professionals' by observing 'micromovements'. Retrieved from https://www.the-sun.com/tech/9269150/ai-detect-humans-smoked-cannabis-alert-medical

[39] The Conversation. (n.d.). Will humans go extinct? For all the existential threats, we'll likely be here for a very long time. Retrieved from https://theconversation.com/will-humans-go-extinct-for-all-the-existential-threats-well-likely-be-here-for-a-very-long-time-135327

On September 29th, 2023, Fox 5 San Diego published an article by Bill Shannon exploring how long humans will be able to inhabit the Earth. A group of researchers from the University of Bristol in England may have provided an answer. According to a paper published this week on nature.com, humanity might only have 250 million years left on Earth before a new supercontinent forms. The research team utilized available data on Earth, such as climate, ocean chemistry, and tectonic plate movement, to simulate the future. The formation of the new supercontinent, dubbed PANGEAULTIMA, will bring about adverse effects, including a hotter sun, increased CO_2 in the atmosphere, and higher temperatures on Earth. This will create vast uninhabitable areas and a scarcity of food sources, making survival difficult for mammals. This is an insight into what the future holds and how much time we have left on Earth. However, most people are not asking this question.

Overall, there are many important factors to consider when it comes to issues of social justice and police accountability. We must approach these issues with an open mind and a willingness to learn and adapt. Only then can we truly make progress toward a more just and equitable society.

The complexities of the American justice system are deeply intertwined with capitalism and the vestiges of racism. At the heart of these intersections is the contentious issue of penal forfeiture. As per the North Carolina Constitution, all penal forfeitures are required to go to the county board of education where the seizure occurred. This provision, while seemingly straightforward, opens a Pandora's box of ethical and legal debates. A case in point is the issue of revenue derived from speeding tickets. In most states, this revenue is distributed across various funds, with a portion often going to court or law enforcement funds, thus inadvertently tying the justice system to the very revenues it generates. This raises questions about transparency, accountability, and the potential for conflict of interest.

Simultaneously, there is an issue of regressive non-tax revenue-raising activities, such as fees, fines, and user charges. These burdens fall disproportionately on those with the lowest incomes, as they are typically imposed as a flat fee regardless of income. This regressive system, coupled with the over-policing of neighborhoods predominantly inhabited by people of color, perpetuates a cycle of police violence and economic disparity.

The debate on whether or not the abolition of police and prisons can stop capitalism is a divisive one. For decades, scholars like Ruth Wilson Gilmore have argued that the only escape from these cycles of violence will be to collectively build popular abolitionist frameworks. In North Carolina, organizations like NCBLOC are working towards this goal, advocating for decolonization and prison abolition as a path to liberation.

Yet, liberation is not just about dismantling oppressive systems. It is also about empowerment, which includes building generational wealth and not relying solely on government resources. This requires a collective effort, a shift in mindset, and a real understanding of what freedom truly means.

The issue of police brutality and its aftermath also plays into this narrative. The deaths of black citizens at the hands of police have led to families resorting to platforms like GoFundMe for financial support, often for burial expenses and legal fees. The millions raised for George Floyd's family, largely by white businesses and individuals, highlight the complexities of sympathy, guilt, racism, and capitalist structures.

The fight for justice extends beyond the criminal system and into the realm of civil rights, most notably the fight for voting rights. The history of voting rights in America is fraught with controversy and struggle, from the Women's Suffrage movement to the battle for voting rights for people of color and felons. The fight for equality and justice is a complex, multifaceted battle, one that is deeply influenced by capitalism, racism, and the architecture of our justice system.

To reimagine North Carolina or any other place, requires a thorough understanding of these intersections and the will to dismantle oppressive structures and replace them with systems of justice and equality.

In an 1890s suffrage meeting in Atlanta, a white suffragist asked a Black man not to appear onstage with her, citing inappropriateness. Such racist strategies, however, proved futile as southern white men were already using discriminatory poll taxes, tests, and lynchings to prevent Black men from voting. It wasn't until 1965, after a series of civil rights marches and protests across the U.S., that Black people finally gained the right to vote. Yet, even after emancipation and military drafts, the fight for voting rights continues today.[40]

In North Carolina, activist groups and organizations continually battle against laws that suppress voting rights. For instance, until 2022, felons in NC were exempt from voting until they had completed all sentencing requirements, including paying restitution fees and finishing probation. Yet, a year later, the NC General Assembly reinstated the original bill, effectively revoking the right to vote, marking a disturbing regression towards the Jim Crow era.[41] This battle for equality cannot be discussed without addressing the issue of gerrymandering, a practice rooted in the early days of the American Republic. Elbridge Gerry, a Founding Father, and the fifth vice-president, signed a bill that infamously redrew the Massachusetts district, favoring his party and setting a precedent for political manipulation of voting districts.

The term "gerrymander" was coined at a Boston dinner party in 1812.[42] More than two centuries later, these tactics

---

[40] History.com. (n.d.). How Early Suffragists Left Black Women Out of Their Fight. Retrieved from https://www.history.com/news/suffragists-vote-black-women

[41] NC General Assembly. (n.d.). GS_160A-168.pdf. https://ncleg.net/

[42] Smithsonian Magazine. (n.d.). Where Did the Term "Gerrymander" Come From? Retrieved from https://www.smithsonianmag.com/history/where-did-term-gerrymander-come-180964118/

persist. In 2023, in North Carolina, Michael Bitzer of Catawba College noted how Republican lawmakers re-engaged in aggressive gerrymandering, using techniques known as "packing" and "cracking." This manipulation either clustered Democratic voters into a few districts where Democratic candidates could amass overwhelming majorities or dispersed Democratic voters into districts with higher numbers of Republican-leaning voters.

The power to draw their own voting gives legislators a dangerous advantage, enabling them to skew the electoral landscape in their favor. This practice is often challenged by various groups and organizations, yet many fail to address the root issue of gerrymandering in their missions. The result is a confusing and often ineffective fight for voting rights and fair representation. The struggle for equality extends into other areas of legislation, too, such as the decriminalization of marijuana. If passed, such a bill could help dismantle the vestiges of Jim Crow laws and the capitalism of the people. This would significantly impact the state's "rainy day" funds and could lead to the elimination of fines, fees, and forfeitures, including unclaimed cash and property.[43] However,

---

[43] WECT. (2022, February 3). North Carolina has nearly a billion in unclaimed cash. How to see if some of it is yours! Retrieved from https://www.wect.com/2022/02/03/north-carolina-has-nearly-billion-unclaimed-cash-how-see-if-some-it-is-yours/

misinformation and a lack of understanding about lawmaking often stymie progress in these areas.

The fight for equal voting rights and fair representation is a complex, ongoing struggle against deeply ingrained systems of oppression and manipulation. To truly achieve equality and justice, we must understand these systems and work diligently to dismantle them.

The future of North Carolina, and indeed the entire country, could be dramatically reshaped through the decriminalization of marijuana and the utilization of advanced technologies like artificial intelligence (AI) and digital currencies.

While the decriminalization of marijuana remains a contentious issue, there is no denying its potential economic benefits. Legalizing and regulating cannabis could create new businesses and jobs, attract tourism, and generate significant tax revenue. Despite these potential advantages, North Carolina, like many other states, hesitates to follow the path of decriminalization, often citing concerns about drug misuse and societal impact.

Surprisingly, the same technology that is transforming industries worldwide could also revolutionize law enforcement and the justice system. AI, with its ability to learn and predict patterns, could potentially be used to detect drug use, identify traffickers, and even uncover planted evidence, helping to dismantle the school-to-prison pipeline.

In one experiment, an AI system was trained to identify cannabis users with an impressive 85% accuracy. Though these results are promising, experts like Joseph Wu from Stanford

University and Mark Chandy from Western University advocate for further research and larger sample sizes to validate the AI's capabilities.

The rise of digital currencies also poses interesting possibilities. Countries distancing themselves from the US, such as the BRICS nations, are exploring the potential of creating their own digital currencies. This move could allow for efficient tracking of funds and transactions, potentially dismantling multibillion-dollar illegal industries like human trafficking, drug trafficking, and gun smuggling.

Digital currencies also promise increased financial transparency, potentially eradicating corporate tax evasion and exposing illicit funds hidden by government officials at various levels. However, while these industries contribute billions to the US economy, the question arises: why doesn't the US utilize digital currencies to track transactions?

The potential ramifications of these technological advances are far-reaching and must be carefully considered from all angles. Activists advocating for survivors and victims of human trafficking, drug trafficking, and gun violence must challenge the government's use of digital currency and other advanced technologies to ensure they are used to promote justice and equality, not to perpetuate existing inequalities and injustices.

The road to a future North Carolina free from oppressive systems may seem daunting, but with the right applications of technology and progressive legislation, it becomes a tangible possibility.

The rise of artificial intelligence (AI) and digital currencies poses complex questions and challenges for activists and advocates alike. Could AI identify individuals involved in illicit activities such as drug and human trafficking? Could digital currencies eradicate corporate tax evasion and expose hidden funds of city, county, and state officials? As we navigate these uncharted territories, we must consider the implications for those advocating for survivors and victims of human trafficking, drug trafficking, and gun violence. As Sam Cooke once sang, "A change is gonna come," but what will this change look like, and where will it leave us?

The increasing prevalence of AI in industries and law enforcement prompts us to consider the future role of human beings in these areas. AI's potential capabilities could render certain professions obsolete, including some forms of activism. As AI begins to dominate, whom can we trust? What will become of activists when their roles are assumed by AI systems?

These questions are particularly pertinent in the context of the ongoing drug crisis. With the rise of dangerous substances like fentanyl, a drug often used to lace marijuana, the debate around drug decriminalization becomes even more complex. If AI policing can identify drug dealers but deems their arrest a low priority, where does this leave activists and advocates? Moreover, the financial aspect of activism cannot be ignored. Many activists rely on their work for their livelihoods. With some staff salaries exceeding $150,000 per year, one might question whether these individuals are capitalizing on the injustices that citizens face.

In the face of these challenges, the future of activism may seem daunting. Still, the fight for justice is a deeply personal one. For many activists, the fight is not just about the broader societal issues but also about their own survival.

The news cycle, filled with stories of heartbreaking violence and injustice, often leaves activists and advocates feeling overwhelmed and disillusioned. Yet, even in the face of such despair, they continue to fight, driven by a deep belief in the interconnectedness of all human beings.

But as the world changes and technologies like AI become more prevalent, activists must reassess their roles. They must grapple with the possibility that the very tools that could help end certain injustices might also render their roles obsolete.

The future is uncertain and filled with possibilities and challenges. Yet, one thing remains clear: the fight for justice and equality will continue in whatever form it takes. Whether marching in the streets or working behind a desk, activists will continue to strive for change, guided by their experiences and the knowledge they have acquired.

"The fight for humanity is everyone's fight for equality."[44]

—Kathy A. Greggs, Co-Founder Fayetteville PACT

---

[44] Goodreads.com. (n.d.). Showing all quotes that contain 'kathy greggs'. Retrieved from https://www.goodreads.com/quotes/search?utf8=√&q=kathy+greggs&commit=Search

As we move forward, we must embrace the changes that come, adapt to new realities, and continue fighting for a world where justice and equality are not just ideals but realities.

Chapter 5: The Mother, The Soldier, and The Activist "The Way Ahead"

In every audio biography, the story always begins before one's birth. Unconventionally, mine started on the cusp of my existence. Carved and created with a unique touch, I was known only to God, the grand artist who created my existence. My life mirrored the lives of many from Camden, New Jersey, yet I yearned to stand apart, to step back into the limelight, not for mere vanity but as a testament to my struggle and survival.

This tale isn't narrated with pride—it's a beacon of hope for those caught between a life of despair and the promise of something wonderful. It's a story that began when I was just 6 ½ years old, a time when my mother had to make a difficult decision that would change our lives forever.

Picture a young girl, innocent and naive, with light skin and a thin frame, her hair a riot of curls, journeying to a place unknown and unfamiliar—Karlsruhe, Germany. Among strangers who resembled me, I felt an unexplainable disconnect. In my tender years, I confessed to my mother that I believed myself to be white, and I desired only to play with white dolls—a stark contrast to my sister, who, with her charming smile, brown skin, and unwavering protectiveness, was my idol. Germany at that time was a cauldron of political unrest, with terrorism and neo-Nazism rearing their ugly heads. On the Army Base, I found myself constantly drawn to the world beyond, seeking to understand the happenings of this foreign land. My companions were children of diverse cultures, yet conspicuously, none were African American.

Every weekend, I would plead with my mother to straighten my hair instead of braiding it. She'd humor me, managing my unruly curls that had a mind of their own. She didn't object to my friendships with Japanese and Vietnamese children either. I once had a black friend in elementary school, but I distanced myself from her because she was always upset and excessively talkative.

Does this sound familiar?

I'm sure it does. A well-kept secret amongst us is the disdain some harbor for loud, ignorant, and irate individuals.

But before I delve into my encounters with racism in Germany, it's essential to confront the internal colorism I once harbored. This is my story, a narrative of my unique journey—the mosaic of my childhood.

www.ingramcontent.com/pod-product-compliance
Lightning Source LLC
LaVergne TN
LVHW051039070526
838201LV00066B/4858